The Roosevelt ancestral home, built on the Hudson in 1826, is known as Hyde Park, after the nearby village of that name. It became a National Historic Site on January 15, 1944.

Roosevelt's America

Franklin Roosevelt at the outset of the politic[al] career which culminated in world leadership.

Roosevelt's America

BY ROBIN McKOWN

Qui plantavit curabit

PUBLISHERS Grosset & Dunlap NEW YORK

To

ALIDA MALKUS

Foreword

The America of Franklin D. Roosevelt's lifetime stretched from the end of the horse-and-buggy era in 1882 to the opening of the atomic age in 1945. It encompassed the Spanish-American War and those larger conflicts labeled World War I and World War II. It embraced the most astounding scientific and technological developments in the history of mankind.

Within those 63 years the automobile evolved from a noisy, sputtering, comic contraption to the modern streamlined models. Man learned to fly, and in time the wonder of it died down and air transportation became commonplace. Electric lighting became practical for everyone, and "city electrification" was followed by "rural electrification." Soon there were electric stoves, washing machines, toasters, irons, vacuum cleaners and other gadgets to make life easier for the American housewife.

In 1886, a German, Herr Heinrich Hertz, transmitted signals without wires from one end of a lecture hall to the other. Ten years later,

Signor Guglielmo Marconi of Italy took out a patent for the wireless method of sending messages through space, and the seeds were sown for the vast industries of radio and television.

The word "radioactivity" was created by radium's discoverer, Marie Curie, in 1898. In 1905 came Albert Einstein's famous equation, showing that energy is equal to mass multiplied by the square of the velocity of light. The New Zealander, Ernest Rutherford, produced experimental proof that the tiny atom, like the vast solar system, was mostly empty space, with an incredibly dense and minute nucleus in the center. The atom nucleus gave its name to nuclear science. In America, in 1942, the first nuclear reactor, which transformed mass into enormous quantities of energy in accordance with Einstein's equation, was set into operation. Peaceful uses of atomic energy, however, were postponed because of wartime exigencies.

Roosevelt's America saw a wide transition in literary tastes from the touching sentimentality of Louisa May Alcott and the romanticism of Richard Harding Davis to the brutal strength of Jack London, the realism of Theodore Dreiser, the class-conscious crusading of Upton Sinclair, the cynicism of H. L. Mencken, the terse sophistication of Ernest Hemingway. The emancipation of women became a reality, and labor unions grew in numbers and strength.

The theories of Sigmund Freud swept the country, and psychoanalysis unfortunately became a parlor pastime. In succession and overlapping came the popularity of jazz, the Charleston, the Big Apple, the Lambeth Walk, swing, and "boogie-woogie." Classical music found a widening audience, and symphony orchestras sprang up in major cities and towns from coast to coast.

The first America which Roosevelt knew was the lovely estate at Hyde Park; his early childhood was bounded in the narrow circle of Duchess County aristocracy. Partly because of the influence of his wife, Eleanor, he became aware of the multitudes of Americans less privileged than he. That he came to identify himself with these multitudes, sharing their dreams and their sorrows, was perhaps due to a terrible illness which left him crippled for life.

He became the 32nd President of the United States in 1933, served an unprecedented three terms and part of a fourth. In these more than twelve years, the man who could not walk alone brought America out of a disastrous depression, inaugurated unemployment insurance, social security, old age pensions, child labor laws, and other social legislation, led the nation to the verge of victory in the most catastrophic war the world had known. To promote his great dream of world peace, he fostered and christened the United Nations, which held its first meeting in San Francisco just 13 days after his death.

Franklin Roosevelt's story is that of a man who achieved greatness because the qualities of greatness were demanded of him. Without him, the course of American history — and world history — would have been drastically different. He left as his heritage his simple and unassailable objective: "to make life better for the average man, woman, and child."

Contents

ACKNOWLEDGMENT

For their courtesy and cooperation in supplying the pictures on the pages indicated, the author gives grateful acknowledgment to the following:

FRANKLIN D. ROOSEVELT LIBRARY: Pages 14, 19, 22, 24, 30, 34, 38, 55, 56, 62.

LOS ALAMOS PHOTO LABORATORY: Page 93 (3 pictures).

FRENCH EMBASSY PRESS AND INFORMATION DIVISION: Page 61.

U. S. ARMY: Pages 73, 78, 79, 80, 81, 82, 84-85, 86-87, 88, 93.

NEW YORK STATE DEPARTMENT OF COMMERCE: Page 40.

NATIONAL CHILD LABOR COMMITTEE: Page 15.

AMERICAN RED CROSS: Pages 75, 77.

EWING GALLOWAY: Pages 27, 83 (Official U. S. Army photo from Ewing Galloway).

CHARLES PHELPS CUSHING: Pages 2-3, 9, 52-53, 68, 90.

WIDE WORLD PHOTOS: Pages 17, 59, 65 (2 pictures), 66, 67, 69, 71, 72 (8 pictures), 89, 91 (4 pictures).

CULVER PICTURES, INC.: Pages 16 (2 pictures), 18, 20, 21, 23, 24, 25, 26, 28, 29, 31, 32, 33, 37, 39, 41, 42-43, 44 (2 pictures), 45, 46, 47, 48, 49, 50, 57, 58, 63, 64, 74, 92, 94-95.

The author would like to give special thanks to Miss Elizabeth Drury and Miss Margaret Suckley, of the Franklin D. Roosevelt Library; to Major Howard G. Stevenson, of the U. S. Army Office of Information; to Miss Pauline Thurman, of the Pan-American Union; to Mr. Richard G. Hewlett, Chief Historian of the Atomic Energy Commission; and to Mrs. Joan Saunders for her research assistance.

Roosevelt's America

I. Young Prince of Hyde Park

*"Remember always that all of us, and you and I especially,
are descended from immigrants and revolutionists."*

"At quarter to nine my Sallie had a splendid large baby boy. He weighs ten pounds without clothes."

The baby's father, James Roosevelt, made this entry in a diary at Hyde Park, N. Y., on January 30, 1882. He named the child after his wife's uncle, Franklin Delano.

The Civil War had been over nearly eighteen years, and it was six years since General George Custer and over 200 of his men lost their lives in the Indian attack by the Little Big Horn River. Ulysses S. Grant, old, sick, penniless and in disgrace, was writing the story of his glorious past. The courtly Chester A. Arthur was in the White House, and Congress was about to pass the Chinese Exclusion Act, to bar Chinese laborers from entering the United States.

The suffragette, Susan B. Anthony, at sixty-two, was still lecturing on woman's right to vote. Bell's telephone and Edison's phonograph were crude instruments barely five years old. The world's first central electric power plant was opening in New York City.

Unemployment had increased and salaries had decreased. New York garment workers, those who had jobs, found five dollars, or sometimes only three, in their weekly pay envelopes. Children, paid almost nothing, commonly worked in coal mines, factories, textile mills, and elsewhere.

But poverty and want were strangers in the childhood world of Franklin Delano Roosevelt. His parents were both wealthy and socially

Reaching up for a paycheck. America had 800,000 working children between 10 and 13. No one bothered to count the younger ones.

...anklin Roosevelt, age five, with his father. In ...youth, James Roosevelt fought for the freedom of Italy with the legions of Garibaldi.

[15]

prominent. The Roosevelts were descendants of a Dutchman, Claes Martensven Van Rosenvelt, who arrived in the New World in the 1640's. Franklin's beautiful and regal young mother, Sara Delano Roosevelt, was of mixed French and Dutch descent, and traced her ancestors to William the Conqueror.

Franklin was an only child and had few playmates his own age, but from his early years he learned to be at ease with very important people. After Grover Cleveland became President, Franklin's father took him for a visit to the White House. "Little man," Mr. Cleveland reportedly told the five-year-old boy, "the one thing I hope for you is that you never become President of the United States." Later Franklin and his father went to see Mark Twain, author of *The Adventures of Tom Sawyer* and *A Connecticut Yankee in King Arthur's Court*. Twain was Franklin's favorite writer for years and influenced his own style of writing.

To call attention to women's right to vote, suffragettes held meetings and parades, went on hunger strikes, endured ridicule and imprisonment.

Franklin's parents lavished on him everything a boy could desire. Hyde Park, a spacious rambling clapboard house overlooking the Hudson River, was his palace. The woods and farmlands around it were his kingdom. He had a dog named Budgy, a Shetland pony, and, later, a Texas quarter horse. He started a stamp collection at the age of eight with some Chinese stamps his mother gave him. This hobby, which he continued all his life, helped him to learn a vast amount about world geography.

When Franklin was eleven his father gave him a gun, with permission to shoot one — and only one — bird of each species on the estate. Soon he had a splendid collection of stuffed birds. His Grandfather Delano was so impressed with the boy's knowledge of bird life that he gave him a life membership in the Museum of Natural History.

In winter there were ice skating, tobogganing, and wild rides down the river in his iceboat, *The Hawk*. Summer meant Campobello, a rocky rugged island nine miles by three, across from Eastport, Maine, and part of the Canadian province of New Brunswick. From his father, Franklin mastered the art of sailing a 51-foot yacht called

President William McKinley was shot by a mentally sick youth, Leon Czolgosz, at Buffalo's Pan-American Exposition on September 6, 1901. He died eight days later.

[16]

the *Half Moon*. His love of the sea led him to read, study, and almost memorize Alfred Mahan's *History of Sea Power*. He learned to swim with as much ease as he walked or ran.

Franklin's early education was by private tutoring. His favorite governess was Mademoiselle Jeanne Sandoz, who taught him to speak and write and *think* in French. He became interested in Egyptian history and wrote a small essay about it: "The working people had nothing . . . The Kings made them work so hard and gave them so little that by wingo! they nearly starved . . ."

Nearly every year Franklin's parents went to Europe, and frequently they took their son with them. The summer he was fourteen he and his tutor, Arthur Dumper, bicycled through the Black Forest in Germany and were arrested four times in one day. Their "crimes" were knocking over a goose, picking cherries, parking their bicycles in a railway station, and cycling after sunset.

In that year of 1896, gold was discovered in the Klondike, starting a mad gold rush to that land of ice and snow. Sober William McKinley, a Republican, won the Presidential election with his promise of "the full dinner pail," over his rival Democratic candidate, the golden-tongued orator, William Jennings Bryan. Almost everywhere streetcars were being propelled by electric motors rather than drawn by horses. The more adventurous American families were sporting "horseless carriages."

In the fall Franklin enrolled at Groton, a boys' school in Massachusetts. Groton students were mostly sons of old Boston and New York families. Franklin was the only Democrat in the entire student body of Republicans. As a Groton student, he slept in a doorless cubicle, rose before seven, took a cold shower every morning, and dressed for dinner in a stiff collar and patent leather boots. The diet was so Spartan that only

One day Mrs. Sara Roosevelt found her ten-year-old son reading the dictionary. When she acted surprised, he commented, "But the dictionary is so interesting!"

packages from home kept actual hunger away.

The dreary routine of his first year was enlivened by a visit of New York Police Commissioner Theodore Roosevelt, a distant cousin of Franklin, who belonged to the Republican branch of the family. Proudly the boy wrote his parents that Cousin Teddy "kept the whole room in an uproar for an hour telling killing stories about policemen." Franklin signed his letters home "F.D.R.," a habit he continued always.

"Cousin Teddy" was Assistant Secretary of the Navy in 1898, when the Spanish-American war broke out. He resigned to organize his celebrated Rough Riders. Franklin, hearing of his cousin's exciting exploits, plotted to run away and enlist. He was thwarted by an attack of measles.

His scholastic record was not spectacular, but he did rather well at debating. On different occasions he argued for the independence of the Philippine Islands, and against annexation of Hawaii. Surprisingly, in view of later events, he mentioned Pearl Harbor, pointing out that "a little inexpensive dredging" would transform it into a valuable naval base.

For a youth of Franklin's social background, Harvard was automatically the next step after Groton. He was eighteen when he entered, a slender, blue-eyed blond giant, six feet one and a half inches tall. Even his pince-nez glasses could not distort his striking good looks.

In Franklin's Freshman year, McKinley was elected President for a second term. Cousin Teddy Roosevelt became Vice-President. A few months later, in 1901, McKinley was assassinated and Franklin's Republican cousin moved into the White House. James Roosevelt had died by that time, and F.D.R.'s mother had moved up to Boston to be near her "darling boy."

At Harvard he lived on the fashionable "Gold Coast" and joined the exclusive Fly and Hasty Pudding Clubs. He tried out for football but failed to make the team, took up rowing and stroked several minor crews. He was still interested in naval matters, and he started a collection of naval pamphlets and prints. He joined the staff of the *Harvard Crimson* as a reporter and became president of this student paper in his Senior year. He was frequently entertained by Boston's blueblood families. Some of them were rather shocked to learn that he was writing letters to southern colleges, urging them to admit Negro students as Harvard did.

During his Harvard years Franklin also re-

Theodore Roosevelt's exploits with the Rough Riders in the Spanish-American War won him wide popularity and insured him the Presidency. He was Franklin's fifth cousin.

At seventeen, Franklin (with straw hat) was manager of the baseball team at the exclusive boy school of Groton, in Massachusetts.

newed acquaintance with a fifth cousin he had seen at irregular intervals since she visited Hyde Park as a small child — the niece of his Cousin Teddy, Anna Eleanor Roosevelt.

Eleanor was an orphan brought up by her grandmother. Her childhood, in contrast to Franklin's, had been lonely and unhappy. In spite of three years' schooling in England, she was shy, naive, and a bit awkward. Though she considered herself an ugly duckling, Franklin found her exceedingly attractive. She had soft golden hair, enormous blue eyes, and a warm, friendly manner.

She was intelligent too, interested in serious things, like politics and social reform. Once Franklin picked her up at the Rivington Street Settlement House, where she was teaching New York slum children "calisthenics and fancy dancing."

In 1903 — the year the Wright brothers made their first successful air flight at Kitty Hawk — Eleanor and Franklin became engaged. Sara Roosevelt, who considered no one good enough for her splendid son, promptly hustled him away on a Caribbean cruise, hoping that time and distance would make him change his mind. Her plan failed for Franklin was in love, deeply and permanently. They were married in New York on St. Patrick's Day, March 17, 1905.

Since Eleanor had no father, Theodore Roosevelt gave her away — and stole the show from bride and bridegroom. It took seventy-five policemen to control the crowd who had come to catch a glimpse of the President. A flock of small boys perched atop a fence called out, "Three cheers for Teddy!" as his carriage passed. The *New York World* noted that the President's niece wore a bridal gown of white satin, a collar of pearls, and a diamond bowknot. Franklin was ignored.

Their honeymoon was postponed so that he could continue his law studies at Columbia University in New York City until June. They left then on a glorious tour through Europe. It was the happiest and most carefree period of their lives. Soon after their return to New York they moved into a house on East 65th Street, which Mrs. Sara Roosevelt had bought for them and had furnished completely. She had taken the house next door for herself. Unable to stop her son's marriage, she had decided to take charge of it.

A few weeks after they were settled, Franklin came home to find his young wife weeping. He asked her gently what the matter was. Still sobbing, she said that she did not like living in a house which was in no way hers and which did not represent the way she wanted to live. It was some years before Eleanor Roosevelt became sufficiently independent to resist the well-meaning domination of her mother-in-law.

Their first child was born in 1906, a beautiful baby girl they named Anna. James came along

Mrs. Sara Roosevelt first opposed her son's marriage to Eleanor, later loaded the newly married couple with advice and presents.

in 1907. That year Franklin was admitted to the bar and took his first job, as a clerk in the law firm of Carter, Ledyard and Milburn. Though he did not care much for his work, the job gave him a chance to meet all sorts of people outside of his mother's social circle.

The 65th Street house in New York was their home, but, children and all, they went to Campobello each summer, while weekends were spent at Hyde Park. Young F.D.R., as people were beginning to call him, was popular in that Duchess County community. In 1910 (the year that a third son, Elliott, was born), a group of politicians summoned him to nearby Poughkeepsie. "How would you like to run for state senator on the Democratic ticket?" they asked him.

He agreed, mainly because it would provide diversion from his boring job. There seemed little chance of his being elected. With one exception there had not been a Democratic senator from that district since 1856. He became really interested only after he started campaigning.

He decided to campaign by automobile, which no one had done before. For the purpose he hired a red Maxwell, without a windshield and without a top, and whizzed down the road at the breathtaking speed of twenty miles an hour. Whenever he met a horse or team — about every half mile or so — he pulled over and stopped, not only the car but the engine as well, so that he had to get out and crank to get started again.

In this way he visited every town and village in Duchess County. He spoke from crossroads, from the tops of haystacks, wherever he could find an audience. He talked to Italian railway workers about the dangers of "bossism," and to farmers he promised what they seemed to want most at the time — a standardized apple barrel. He realized he had the gift of making friends when he put his mind to it, but he was still surprised when he won — by a narrow margin of 1,140 votes.

In the same year as Franklin Roosevelt's first political victory, Halley's Comet arrived for its once-in-every-seventy-five-year performance before Earth's stargazers. The appearance of this extraordinarily brilliant heavenly body was like an omen, heralding the arrival of a new and great world leader.

At Kitty Hawk, North Carolina, on December 17, 1903, brothers Orville and Wilbur Wright launched the first controlled and sustained flight in a power-driven airplane.

II. A Widening Horizon

"Public office means serving the public and nobody else."

In 1911, Tammany Hall had a stranglehold on Democratic politics, not only in New York City but throughout the state. "You can't fight Tammany," was an axiom among Democratic politicians who wanted to get ahead. Yet almost the first thing that Franklin Roosevelt did as state senator was to start a fight with this powerful organization.

Charles F. Murphy, Tammany boss, had announced his support of wealthy William F. Sheehan as United States Senator from New York. In Roosevelt's opinion, "Blue-eyed Billy" Sheehan had no qualifications worthy of this important post, and his nomination could only bring disgrace on the Democratic Party. Franklin invited a group of progressive Democrats to a meeting at the large brownstone house in Albany which he and Eleanor had rented, explained how he felt, and asked them if they would help to oppose Sheehan. Enough of this group were willing to follow his leadership to make it worth while to go ahead.

The battle between the marshalled forces of Tammany and the inexperienced state senator and his supporters lasted ten weeks. As a result, Tammany dropped "Blue-eyed Billy," and an-

other candidate was chosen. It was not a major victory, but F.D.R. had shown that he meant what he said when he had promised to oppose "bossism."

Teddy Roosevelt, back from lion hunting in Africa, sent a letter of congratulation. "The young man just elected as state senator from a safe Republican district in New York will bear watching," said the Governor of New Jersey, a former Princeton University president named Woodrow Wilson.

A hard-boiled Albany newspaperman, Louis McHenry Howe, had once thought the new state senator was "a spoiled, silk pants sort of guy."

TAMMANY IN FOR IT
From the *Journal* (Minneapolis)

Tammany was originally a patriotic society dedicated to Jeffersonian democracy. Over the years it became scarred with scandal.

F.D.R. at his desk in the Navy Department. He was young, ambitious, energetic, confident, popular, and a splendid athlete. The future stretched ahead of him like a golden promise.

[23]

As Governor of New Jersey, Woodrow Wilson inspired Franklin Roosevelt with his talk of freeing the government from the hands of the few and entrusting it to the people.

From Albany newspaperman, Louis McHenry Howe, Franklin Roosevelt learned his way through the labyrinth of political intrigue.

Now he changed his mind: "The boy's got courage!" Howe was a gnome-like little man, who smoked cigarettes constantly, secretly wrote poetry, and was an expert on Albany politics. He fell into the habit of dropping into the Roosevelt home regularly, never saying much but watching closely what went on there.

Tammany men, veterans in rough-and-tumble politics, now realized that the young socialite they had taken for a docile lamb was a lion in disguise. Among themselves they gave grudging admiration to this Harvard-bred young man with the softly modulated voice, and more than ever they realized that a "Democratic Roosevelt" was too valuable a property to lose.

The duties of a state senator proved rather dull on the whole, but when Roosevelt was made chairman of the Forest, Fish and Game Committee, he found a cause worth fighting for. Heart and soul, he threw himself into a crusade to save New York's forests from the greed of logging companies and to preserve her wild life from wanton destruction. Why should a few have the right to monopolize Nature's gifts to all? At this time he began to think in terms of social planning, of a society whose benefits would be for the many rather than for the few.

He went to New Jersey to see Governor Woodrow Wilson, a dignified, remote man of great sincerity and integrity. It was a relief for F.D.R. to talk to someone dedicated to world peace and the welfare of the American people. In New York he organized Democrats to support Wilson's candidacy for President, and he attended the exciting Baltimore Convention when Wilson was nominated.

Franklin's own re-election came up that fall of 1912, but an attack of typhoid fever kept him from campaigning. Louis Howe offered to manage his campaign for him. Using publicity methods new to Duchess County, he flooded the district with multigraphed letters, posters, and advertisements, proclaiming Roosevelt as "Labor's Best Friend in Albany" and "Needed in the Fight for Conservation." The techniques worked, and Roosevelt won by a large majority.

Howe had in his head the odd notion that Franklin Roosevelt would one day occupy the top place in the United States government. Henceforth he began letters and memos to him: "Most Revered Future President."

That was the year the "unsinkable" *Titanic,* the world's largest liner, struck an iceberg and sank in the North Atlantic, at the cost of 1000 lives. "Wireless telegraphy" — not yet called radio — brought aid to some who might otherwise have perished.

Roosevelt went to Washington to attend Wilson's Inauguration in March of 1913. By chance, he ran into Josephus Daniels, former editor of the *Raleigh News and Observer,* whom he had met in Baltimore the year before. Daniels had just been appointed Secretary of the Navy, and Roosevelt offered his congratulations.

"How would you like to come to Washington as Assistant Secretary of the Navy?" Daniels asked unexpectedly.

Franklin had loved the sea ever since his first summers at Campobello. He knew as much about navigation, from practice and study, as many navy men. Already he had a sizable collection of naval prints and ship models, along with a total of 9,872 pamphlets on the Navy — of which he had read all but one catalog. There was only one answer to Daniels' offer:

"It would please me better than anything in the world."

He was sworn in on March 17, 1913, his eighth wedding anniversary.

The America over which Woodrow Wilson had

Josephus Daniels, Secretary of the Navy, with his young assistant.

assumed leadership had a population of some 94,000,000 persons. A million immigrants were arriving annually. The self-starter had replaced the crank on automobiles, and thousands were taking to the highways in Model-T Fords. Women's skirts were still ankle length; and hats were high and large. The great French actress, Sarah Bernhardt made her first motion pictures, *Queen Elizabeth* and *Camille.* The reading public swung the pendulum between Zane Grey's *Riders of the Purple Sage* and Theodore Dreiser's *The Financier.* In New York, a dramatization of *Little*

Women was hailed by critics for its fresh and wholesome qualities.

J. Pierpont Morgan gave art treasures valued at fifty million dollars to the Metropolitan Museum of Art, and John D. Rockefeller, Jr. donated a million dollars to set up a psychological laboratory "to save women from a life of crime." For the average worker times were hard, but there were high hopes that the new "college professor President" would lead them to a better life. There was no personal income tax, and the national debt amounted to only $11 per person.

In Washington, the Roosevelts moved into the house where Cousin Teddy had lived before he stepped up to the White House. Sara Roosevelt helped them get settled, as she always did. When two more sons were born — Franklin Jr., in 1914, and John Aspinwall, in 1916, they found a larger home. To economize, Roosevelt walked to his tiny office in the State, War and Navy Building. His wife found this rather amusing since money meant nothing to him if he wanted to buy an item for one of his collections. When there were extra expenses, such as a $223 doctor's bill for the children's ear troubles, Sara Roosevelt came to the rescue. She was always most generous with her adored grandchildren. Sometimes it seemed to Eleanor that she spoiled them.

Henry Ford in the first automobile he ever built. On December 4, 1915, Ford's "peace ship" sailed to Europe "to get the boys out of the trenches by Christmas," but failed in its purpose.

"Roosevelts believe in large families." There were five children in this Roosevelt family (left to right) Anna, Franklin D. Jr., James, John, Elliott.

On April 2, 1917, President Woodrow Wilson, after long wrestling with his conscience, asked Congress for a declaration of war against Germany.

Theoretically, F.D.R.'s duty was to supervise the business affairs of the Navy, but he had soon enlarged his responsibilities. He brought in Louis Howe as his assistant, and the two of them worked closely together. The first step was to make a survey of the American Navy. It was vastly overrated, Roosevelt discovered. "We are supposed to have 36 or 37 battleships built or building," he wrote. "We have 16 . . ." A number of these ships were laid up for lack of crews. "We have a coastline of 2000 miles; only 200 miles are pro-

tected by coast defense guns . . . We must create a navy not only to protect our shores and our own possessions but our merchant ships in time of war."

Navy yards were in bad shape, and he visited them from coast to coast to judge whether they should be improved or abandoned. He initiated more efficient methods of purchasing supplies, changed the basis of promotion for naval officers from length of service to merit, campaigned to have all sailors learn to swim — there had been too many drownings. When he discovered the shipyard wage scale was unjust, he persuaded his chief to put wages under his jurisdiction and thereupon set up a system of collective bargaining.

He adored every part of his job, the 17-gun salute when he visited the fleet, the friendships with naval officers, the ships, the naval talk. "I now find my vocation combined with my avocation in the most delightful ways," he said.

A friend warned Josephus Daniels that "every person named Roosevelt wants to run everything." The Secretary of the Navy, a genial, middle-aged man, was not worried. "Any man who is afraid his assistant will supplant him confesses that he doesn't think he's big enough for his job."

"How young, how debonair," he said wistfully of Roosevelt.

When war broke out in Europe in July, 1914, Roosevelt was convinced that "the most terrible drama in history was about to be enacted." He was exasperated that Daniels and Woodrow Wilson and Congress did not seem to grasp the threat to America of the European war. To Eleanor, he wrote, "I just know I shall do some awful un-neutral thing before I get through." Only later would he understand the hesitation of his superiors to give Germany any excuse for aggression.

In May, 1915, a German submarine torpedoed the unarmed British liner *Lusitania*. Nearly 1200 men, women, and children were drowned, including 114 Americans. President Wilson's strong note of protest to Germany brought an evasive reply. After this outrage, there was no doubt that America must be prepared for the worst.

Even before Congress voted to spend the money, the energetic Assistant Secretary of the Navy was ordering millions of dollars' worth of supplies for new battleships and cruisers. Later he said wryly that he could have been "sent to jail for 999 years" for all the regulations he bypassed.

Josephus Daniels sent him to Haiti early in 1917, where American marines had been stationed after a revolutionary outburst two years before. In company with Major-General Smedley D. Butler, he toured the country, charming the Haitians with his courtesy and the respect he paid their traditions of independence.

Germany's acts of provocation continued. Wilson finally called a special session of Congress. "Right is more precious than peace," he told the members. Congress then passed a resolution recognizing a state of war with Germany.

Roosevelt doubled his activities. He arranged to have cantonments built to handle the increased navy personnel, high-pressure shipyard officials to turn out the needed tonnage faster, helped design a 110-foot submarine chaser, which was soon

Woodrow Wilson leading a Liberty Bond parade.

being produced in quantity and sent across the Atlantic to fight the German U-boats. He suggested a mine barrage across the neck of the North Sea from the Orkney Islands to Norway to fence submarines in their lair. British and American admirals said it could not be done. The barrage, laid in the spring of 1918, was a final blow to the morale of the U-boat crews.

Americans, who had re-elected Wilson on the grounds that "He kept us out of war," soon rallied to the call of patriotism. "Lafayette, we are here," and "Give until it hurts," were the war slogans. Women knitted socks, scarfs, gloves to keep "soldier boys" warm while they were fighting the "Hun." Children saved their pennies to buy thrift stamps. Motion picture stars Marie Dressler, Charlie Chaplin, Douglas Fairbanks, and Mary Pickford spoke at "Liberty Bond" rallies.

A rash of new songs was heard: "Over There,"

"You're in the Army Now," "Pack Up Your Troubles in Your Old Kit Bag."

A Woman's Reserve in the U.S. Naval Reserve was authorized after Josephus Daniels asked, "Is there any law that says a yeoman must be a man?" Some 11,000 yeomanettes were recruited.

Wives and mothers hung small banners in their front windows with a blue star for each fighting member of the family. As the months passed, more and more of the blue stars were changed for gold ones — a symbol of someone who had given his life for his country.

Franklin Roosevelt asked permission to resign his post and join the armed forces. Josephus Daniels relayed the request to Wilson. "Tell the young man," said the President, "that his only and best war service is to stay where he is."

Later Daniels sent Roosevelt on a European

In 1918, F.D.R. asked permission to resign his Navy post and join the armed forces. "Tell the young man," President Wilson said to Secretary Daniels, "that his only and best war service is to stay where he is."

inspection trip. He ignored the safe tour a naval attaché had arranged for him. Instead, he went to devastated Dünkirk, on to Paris, and after that as close to the front as he could. He saw Château-Thierry, Belleau Wood, and Verdun; he was under enemy fire and came within a mile of the German lines. "I saw blood running from the wounded . . . men coughing out their gassed lungs . . . the dead in the mud . . . two hundred limping, exhausted men come out of the line — the survivors of a regiment of one thousand that went forward 48 hours before . . ."

He saw war for the first time in terms of human suffering, and he hated it.

On the voyage home, Franklin came down with double pneumonia and it was October before he was able to return to Washington. A month later, on November 11, the Armistice was signed. The "war to end wars" was over at last. In every American city people poured into the streets, laughing and cheering and embracing total strangers.

Roosevelt stayed on at his post as Assistant Secretary of the Navy until 1920. That year he was nominated as Vice-President by the Democratic Party on the basis of his navy record. The Presidential candidate was James Cox. Wilson was ill due in part to his disappointment at the lack of interest shown by Congress and the American people in the League of Nations, which he had fought to make a part of the Treaty of Versailles between the Allies and a defeated Germany. The two candidates promised Wilson to make the League of Nations the most important issue of their campaign.

The cross-country campaign was an exciting adventure for Roosevelt, the more so because this was the first time that women could vote in a Presidential election. But the Democrats were defeated overwhelmingly. Warren Harding, a likable Ohioan, became President of the United States, with Calvin Coolidge, former Governor of Massachusetts, as Vice-President. For Roosevelt the worst thing about their defeat was that with it went the last hope for American acceptance of the League of Nations.

It was two years after the Armistice, and postwar America was swamped with troubles. Wartime wages could no longer be paid, and nationwide strikes broke out. Veterans, coming home to find their old jobs filled, were bitter at the "war profiteers" who had grown fat while they risked their lives.

In post-war America, youth was enjoying a fling. Young women shortened their skirts, bobbed their hair, wore lipstick. Some even smoked cigarettes.

The Prohibition Act, a wartime measure forbidding the sale of intoxicating liquors, was replaced by the Eighteenth Amendment. "See America Thirst," people wisecracked. Almost immediately the bootlegger appeared and with him the speakeasy and the gangster. Everyone was reading F. Scott Fitzgerald's *This Side of Paradise,* which gave a picture of what was called either "The Flapper Age" or "The Lost Generation."

Never again, Americans were saying, would they get mixed up in a foreign war.

III. Fight Against Affliction

"Men are not prisoners of fate, but only prisoners of their own minds."

On the 10th of August, 1921, Franklin Roosevelt took his family for a sail off their island home, Campobello, in his sloop, the *Vireo*. The day was lovely and clear; the tang of salt was in the air. It was a welcome relief from the sweltering New York heat, where he had been working up until a few days before in his new law office. This was his first real vacation since the war. He intended to devote it to getting better acquainted with his offspring.

The "chicks," he and Eleanor called their fast-growing family. Anna, the oldest, was fifteen now, a beautiful girl with long golden hair. Jimmy, at 13, would soon be going back to Groton, where F.D.R. had gone before him. Elliott was ten, Franklin, or "Brud," was seven, and the youngest, Johnny, just five. It was great fun for Roosevelt to teach his sons to manage the sloop, as his own father had done for him.

As they were skirting along the coast of a neighboring island on their way back, they caught sight of a gray spiral of smoke. A forest fire! All excitement, they landed the craft, waded over the rocks and up the coast. The children were enough like their father to feel it their duty to prevent destruction of woodland. It was not a big fire,

but by the time they had beat out the flames with evergreen boughs they were hot, dirty, and smarting with spark-burns.

When they reached their own island, the father proposed a swim in an inland lake. It was a couple of miles distant; they raced all the way. Later, Roosevelt took another plunge by himself, in the icy waters of the Bay of Fundy.

Since the island of Campobello was part of Canadian New Brunswick, it seemed fitting that the Roosevelts should fly both Canadian and American flags in front of their country house.

...anklin Roosevelt, aboard the sloop VIREO off ...e shores of Campobello, instructing his sons, James and Elliott, in the art of sailing.

[33]

A batch of mail was waiting for him at home. Still in his wet bathing suit, he sat down, impatient to read it. Suddenly he felt strangely tired, more so than ever in his life before. Eleanor, fearing he had caught a chill, made him go to bed.

He had planned to take the "chicks" camping the next day, but a fever, combined with unusual pains in his back and legs, kept him in bed. The day after that he could not get up at all. Paralysis had set in, spreading from his legs to his back and arms. Louis Howe's wife Grace, who was staying on the island with her children, sent a telegram to her husband. He came at once. Eleanor summoned two different doctors from the Maine coast. They could give no immediate diagnosis, but one of them, on the theory that a blood clot was causing the paralysis, advised massage.

Louis and Eleanor took turns massaging him

The entire Roosevelt family at Campobello. Before his polio attack, F.D.R. took the lead in water sports and "paper chases" along the cliffs.

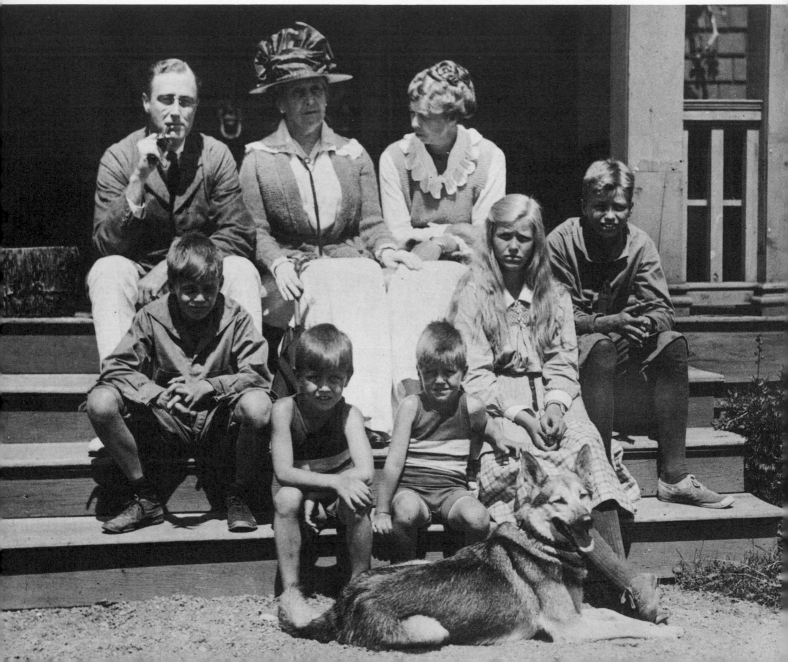

the next few days, but no matter how gentle they tried to be they caused him excruciating pain. Nor did his condition improve. He kept up a brave front to his wife. To Howe, he said, "I don't know what's the matter with me, Louis. I just don't know."

A correct diagnosis was finally made by Dr. Robert W. Lovett, a specialist from Boston. The athletic and husky Franklin Roosevelt was suffering from poliomyelitis — infantile paralysis — a disease more common in children than adults. When Roosevelt learned the truth, his first thought was of the "chicks." The doctor could reassure him that if they had escaped thus far, the danger of contagion was slight. He passed the next weeks in acute agony. His wife or Louis watched at his bedside, night and day.

In mid-September, Dr. Lovett gave permission for the patient to be transferred to New York. Louis Howe took charge of transporting him by stretcher, across the bay and to a private railway car which was waiting for them. The children accompanied the sad procession. They were bewildered by the catastrophe which had deprived them of their father and playmate, and watched, heartbroken, as servants slipped patient and stretcher through a railway car window. They could see him in the train, lying flat, with his feet higher than his head. Then, as the train pulled out, he caught sight of them, and his face burst into a radiant smile. They were reassured that everything would be all right.

The next six weeks Roosevelt spent in the New York Presbyterian Hospital, in the charge of a brilliant young specialist, Dr. George Draper. Louis Howe, to forestall any unpleasant rumors that might hurt his chief's political career, released a short item to the *New York Times*. It said only that F. D. Roosevelt was ill of poliomyelitis, that the use of his legs was affected, but

that he was recovering. The truth was that he could not even sit up, and the doctors feared he would never be able to do so. To ease his pain, they gave him mild opiates.

When did he first accept the fact that he was not going to wake in the morning and find his malady had passed? When did he realize how slim were the chances of recovery? There must certainly have been days of black despair. To his friends and family, he revealed a stubborn cheerfulness. Nurses and doctors were impressed with his courage, yet worried about him. On October 28, he was discharged and allowed to return to his New York home — in a wheel chair. His grim hospital record read: "Not improving."

Very little was then known about polio, but specialists agreed that affected muscles must be taught to work again. The "teaching" could be done only by the patient. It was a great relief to Franklin to know that he could do something himself. As movement returned to his arms, he spent long hours hauling himself up by a sort of overhead trapeze, in the hope of strengthening his back muscles.

For weeks it was still touch and go. In November he had a relapse. His eyes began to hurt and briefly it was feared he might be losing his eyesight. At a time when things looked blackest, when he seemed doomed to spend the rest of his life in bed, the paralysis released its hold on his back. At least, he was able to sit up. Never had he had more cause for rejoicing.

To strengthen his torso, the former athlete took to crawling around the floor of his bedroom like a baby. Next he learned to pull himself up the stairway, one step at a time. Whenever he did this he made his family or Louis watch him, and kept up a steady stream of conversation about other matters, as if to prove to them and himself that he was doing nothing out of the ordinary.

Later he was fitted with steel braces, heavy and uncomfortable contraptions which made it possible for him to stand erect. With braces and crutches, he practiced until he could drag himself along for a few steps. It required enormous muscular effort, more than he had ever expended on any form of sport.

Throughout his ordeal, Eleanor was a constant source of strength. Sara Roosevelt wanted him to retire permanently to Hyde Park, to lead the life of an invalid country gentleman in a wheel chair. Eleanor opposed her mother-in-law with every method at her command. Both she and Louis were positive that Franklin Roosevelt, crippled or not, still had a great deal to offer the world. For his sake and for their own, they were not going to let him give up.

He never walked again without support. He could never stand without his braces or someone on whom to lean. Alone, he could not even rise from a chair or sit down, without great effort. All his life he was plagued with the major and minor inconveniences caused by his useless legs. But gradually he improved enough to take up some of his former interests.

Marguerite Le Hand, a young woman who had done some temporary work for him during his campaign with James Cox, joined the household as his permanent secretary. "Missy," as the family called her, was attractive, charming, efficient, and as sensitive to his needs as if he had been her brother. With her assistance, he carried out plans for the Woodrow Wilson Foundation, an organization dedicated to Wilson's ideals of world cooperation. Louis Howe lived with them too, most of the time. It was he who convinced his chief that his political career was not over.

Less than a year after Franklin was stricken, some of his Democrat friends came to see him. They wanted him to run for Governor of New York State in 1922. The proposal was wonderful for his spirits, but he rejected it. Instead, he proposed they run Al Smith, who had already done a fine job as governor for the 1918-1920 term. They took his advice, and Al triumphed over his Republican rival by a wide majority.

Al Smith had been brought up by a widowed mother in the slums of New York City. He had known poverty and hunger. For a time he had worked twelve hours a day at an underpaid job for the Fulton Fish Market. Firsthand, he knew the dreams and the needs of America's poor. Mrs. Sara Roosevelt considered Al Smith uncouth, an unfit companion for her son, but F.D.R. had great respect for this "knight in the brown derby with the cocked cigar." As for the people of New York, they took him to their hearts as one of their own.

By 1924, some of the Democrats, Franklin Roosevelt among them, decided that Al Smith was Presidential material. F.D.R. agreed to make the nomination speech at the Democratic National Convention, which was being held in the vast Madison Square Garden. It was his first public appearance since his illness.

Until the time came for him to speak, he sat in his wheel chair with the other New York delegates. Then his tall young son Jimmy helped him to his crutches and fastened the steel braces on his legs. Together they walked slowly up the center of the aisle and onto the platform by a ramp. The crowds recognized him and cheered. He handed his crutches to Jimmy, pulled himself erect with both hands on the lectern, and began to speak.

"Corruption will be the overshadowing issue of this campaign," he said, and, "Our candidate has a record of law enforcement; he stands for the whole Constitution." Roosevelt talked for thirty-five minutes and then he named Al Smith.

Learning to manipulate crutches was his first step toward physical rehabilitation.
At far right is Al Smith, whom F.D.R.'s Madison Square Garden speech immor-
talized as the "Happy Warrior."

"He is the Happy Warrior of the political battle-field," he concluded.

Madison Square Garden went wild at that moment. The cheering lasted for one hour and thir-teen minutes. Their acclaim was in reality for the man who had made such a remarkable comeback from physical incapacity. Al Smith did not get the nomination. It went to John W. Davis, who later was defeated by the Republican Party's candi-date, Herbert Hoover. But Roosevelt, for his share in the Convention, emerged as the most impor-tant man in the Democratic Party, and his "Happy Warrior" speech went down in history.

He had done considerable swimming since his

A conference at Roosevelt's Warm Springs cottage. Herbert Lehman sits at left of F.D.R. Samuel Rosenman is standing by the fireplace.

polio attack and had found it made him feel better. In 1923, he took a long cruise in the Florida waters, and returned tanned and healthy-looking.

"The water put me where I am, and the water has to bring me back," he shouted once when he was swimming in the pool of his Hyde Park neighbors, the Vincent Astors.

Shortly after the Convention he received a letter from a friend, George W. Peabody, which interested him greatly. Peabody owned a dilapidated hotel with a swimming pool, in Warm Springs,

Georgia. He thought Roosevelt should know about a young southern lad named Louis Joseph, who also had been crippled with polio. Joseph had been swimming in the Warm Springs pool for some two years and was now able to walk with the aid of only a cane.

If Joseph had derived so much benefit from the Warm Springs water, might it not help Roosevelt too?

Like many other chronic invalids, F.D.R. was willing to try almost anything. As soon as he could manage it, he took a trip to Warm Springs to test the waters himself.

The pool was fed by a subterranean spring with a constant temperature of about 88 degrees. The water was heavy with mineral salts, and one could stay in it several hours without feeling fatigue. Roosevelt stayed six weeks at the Springs, going swimming every day. In that time he made more progress than in the previous three years.

Contrary to his wishes, there was considerable publicity about his experiment. Other invalids arrived, many without funds, hoping for a miracle. Roosevelt looked after them as though they were part of his family, as indeed they were in one way.

The healthy guests at the hotel became alarmed, afraid they would "catch something" if they bathed in the same pool with the sufferers. Gaily, F.D.R. arranged that "his gang" would eat at a separate table. Soon he had a second pool built, for their exclusive use. With the local physician he worked out a series of underwater exercises which he taught them with careful patience. "Dr. Roosevelt," they began to call him.

By 1925, Warm Springs had 23 polio patients. Eventually, Roosevelt bought the entire property as a hydro-therapeutic center. It was incorporated as the non-profit-making Georgia Warm Springs Foundation. To it he donated or loaned a large part of his own personal fortune.

He could not ever undo the catastrophe that had befallen him. He could and did learn from it, and adapt himself to it. There were undeniable advantages. He had a good excuse to avoid boring social functions or interminable dinner parties. He had time to think. What he had once called thinking, he decided, was merely "looking out of the window." The impetuous young man who had turned the Navy upside down in his zeal to get things done fast learned diplomacy and patience.

Newspapermen were struck with his lack of self-consciousness and self-pity. "No sob stuff," he told them firmly. His good humor and serenity amazed everyone.

Even more profound a change was his increasing interest in ordinary, everyday human beings who did not, like his mother, belong to high society. He was, physically at least, one of the underprivileged himself now. Their troubles became his troubles. Instead of shutting himself off from the world, friendliness bubbled out of him from a source as inexhaustible as that of the Warm Springs water.

A woman once asked Mrs. Roosevelt, "Do you think your husband's illness affected his mind?"

"Yes, I think it did," she said thoughtfully. "I think it made him more sensitive to the feelings of people."

The mineral waters of Warm Springs had no special magic to cure polio, but long hours of swimming and water exercises wrought a vast improvement.

IV. When F.D.R. Was Governor

*"I am very mindful of the fact that I am the Governor,
not just of Democrats, but of Republicans and all other
citizens of the State."*

The Democratic Party held its State Convention in Rochester in the fall of 1928, for the purpose of choosing a candidate for Governor of New York State. Al Smith was completing his fourth term in that post and was at last candidate again for President. He had put some pressure on F.D.R. to accept the governorship nomination, feeling it would help him to have Roosevelt on the same ticket. Franklin had said definitely no. He was at Warm Springs, where he intended to spend the winter. Eleanor had gone to the Convention in his place.

It was eight years since he had campaigned for public office, eight years in which, aside from his Happy Warrior speech, he had made few public appearances. Much had happened in that time.

A 1924 law had set up a quota system to limit the stream of immigrants to American shores. By the Johnson Act, in the same year, all Japanese immigrants were excluded, which caused considerable resentment on the part of Japan. In 1925 General "Billy" Mitchell was demoted and court-martialed for criticizing the neglect of air power by military and naval leaders. And in Dayton, Tennessee, the great lawyer, Clarence Darrow, brilliantly but unsuccessfully defended, against

William Jennings Bryan, a young biology teacher charged with teaching evolution to his students. In 1927, Charles Lindbergh made the first solo flight across the Atlantic in the *Spirit of St. Louis*.

Al Capone and other gangsters had turned bootlegging into a monstrous industry, whose business methods were murder and terror. A crop of American writers had sprung into prominence:

Charles Lindbergh's solo flight across the Atlantic made him America's darling and a world hero. Much later he and the America First Committee opposed F.D.R.'s war policy.

om January, 1929, to March, 1933, the stately ecutive Mansion at Albany, New York, was the home of the tumultuous Roosevelt family.

[41]

Sherwood Anderson, John Dos Passos, Ernest Hemingway. Around 25,000,000 automobiles were registered in the United States.

Franklin Roosevelt had not given up his political interests, but he was in no hurry as yet to assume a major role in public affairs. He still clung to the hope that Warm Springs could put life back into his wasted legs. He had once, though only once, walked with braces a few steps unaided.

At the Rochester Convention, time was running short and there was still no candidate for the governorship. On October 2, 1928, while F.D.R. was swimming in the pool, Al Smith put in a long distance call for him. Roosevelt sent back word that he was on a picnic. More calls came, and he ignored them all. A telegram arrived from his married daughter Anna. "Go ahead and take it," it read, meaning the nomination. He wired back, "You ought to be spanked."

Late that evening Eleanor called him from Rochester. Her husband's friends had been hounding her all day, trying to get her to use her influence on her husband. She had firmly refused to do so, but had at last agreed to get him on the phone. As soon as she heard his voice, she let Al Smith speak to him.

"Frank, would you decline if you were nominated?" Al asked.

Roosevelt hesitated briefly, and Al took his hesitation for an affirmative. "Good," he said, and hung up. The next day the papers announced that Franklin D. Roosevelt had been nominated for governor. He must have realized that this nomination meant an end to his hope of ever staying at Warm Springs long enough to effect a cure.

Reluctant as he had been to accept it, he had the time of his life in the campaign. Once more he barnstormed the state by automobile, but now he had a large staff and two buses to accompany

A campaign rally, Roosevelt on the speaker's sta

him, one for newspapermen and the other for stenographers and mimeograph machine operators. He drew up to the side of the road to dictate his speeches, and the operators ran off copies for the press in the moving bus.

t to right: Thomas H. Cullen, James Farley, Ed Flynn.

The opposition tried to make capital of his handicap. It was cruel, they said, to inflict campaigning on "the unfortunate sick man." At a big night meeting in Troy, Roosevelt recited the miles he had traveled that day, the towns he had covered, the number of speeches he had made. "Too bad about the unfortunate sick man, isn't it?" he concluded with a disarming grin. His audience applauded wildly.

His campaign speeches were in simple language anyone could understand. "I am going to talk about a very wet subject," he began one night, and went on to speak, not about prohibition, but about the need for state ownership of the St. Lawrence Water Project, so that farmers could have cheap electricity. He spoke out against racial and religious intolerance, reminding folks how he had watched stretchers of wounded American boys being carried to the rear on the battlefields of World War I: "Somehow in those days people were not asking to what church those American boys belonged . . ."

Wherever a crowd gathered, he spoke from the back of his car — standing up. He and his staff had learned to help him in such a way that hardly anyone noticed he could not get up or sit down unaided. Sometimes he had to be carried up the back stairs of a lecture hall, and there were a few falls and mishaps. But by the time he appeared on the platform, he always managed to look unruffled and self-confident, and he took discomfort and inconvenience in his stride. "If I could campaign for another six months, I could throw away my cane," he cried exultantly to his friends.

He knew, as did his colleagues, how slim were his chances of winning.

The post-war depression had subsided. The stock market was booming. Some million Americans in all walks of life — plumbers, secretaries, domestic servants, grocers, factory workers, widows and old people — were investing their savings in stocks, confident of getting rich quickly. The dour New Englander, President Calvin Coolidge, was given credit for the discovery of a mystic formula for continued prosperity. Largely ignored

Calvin Coolidge   *Herbert Hoover*

were the few conservative bankers who muttered that whatever went up had to come down and that stocks were no exception.

Coolidge had said, with finality, "I do not choose to run for re-election in 1928." As his successor, the Republicans chose Herbert Hoover, former United States Food Administrator and Director of Belgian Food Relief.

Roosevelt heard the election returns in New York City's Biltmore Hotel. The country went more solidly Republican than the most pessimistic Democrats had foreseen. Al Smith even failed to get the electoral vote of his beloved New York, losing overwhelmingly to Hoover. Until almost all the returns were in, it looked as though F.D.R. had been defeated too. He won by a narrow margin of less than 25,000 votes. Thereafter he referred to himself as "one-half of one per cent governor."

The Roosevelts moved into the big Victorian-style Executive Mansion in Albany, the state capital, in January, 1929. James was twenty-one now and a Harvard student. Part of the time Roosevelt's first grandchild, the little daughter of Anna and her husband, Curtis Dall, stayed with them. With so many young people, the gloomy high-ceilinged rooms were filled with noise and

laughter. Nearly always guests came to dinner, on official or semi-official business, and the guest rooms were usually full. There were good times in the Executive Mansion, but there was hard work too.

Al Smith had expected that F.D.R. would keep in office his own special friends, but the new governor insisted on appointing men of his own choice. Smith was resentful and a rift began between the two men which slowly widened.

Roosevelt appointed the invaluable Louis Howe as his Chief of Staff. Miss Frances Perkins, who had an excellent social welfare background, became Chairman of the State Department of Labor. To assist Miss Le Hand in secretarial duties, he brought in another efficient young woman, Grace Tully.

He initiated a practice of calling on experts when he needed information on special subjects. To learn the legal procedure for getting the cheap electricity he had promised his rural voters, he invited Felix Frankfurter, of the Harvard Law School, to Albany. Henry Morgenthau, Jr., a Duchess County neighbor, became his adviser on agricultural matters. Other experts on his staff were Raymond Moley, Columbia professor, Samuel Rosenman (later Judge Rosenman of the New York Supreme Court), Jim Farley, and Ed Flynn.

To the State Assembly, during his first months in office he presented measures on unemployment insurance, old age pensions, and guarantees for the rights of labor. When they balked at such unusual legislation, he started his "Fireside Chats" to the people of New York. Speaking to his radio audience as informally as if he were a guest chatting in their living rooms, he told them what he was trying to do for them, how he was going about it, and what difficulties he faced. Soon letters from his constituents flooded the state offices and the Assembly had to take notice.

While Governor of New York, F.D.R. inaugurated his famous Fireside Chats to the people. Behind him, one of his model ship collection.

He had been in office ten months when, in October, 1929, the stock market crashed. By October 29, which became known as "Black Thursday," the floor of the stock exchange was chaos. Orders to sell came in faster than it was humanly possible to record — and there was no one to buy. Securities fell to half, a third, a quarter their former prices. Small investors and large ones found themselves holding near-worthless certificates. Day after day newspapers printed grim lists of suicides. Almost immediately three million were added to the ranks of the unemployed.

As the news grew worse, the Republican Party was blamed for the disaster, just as it had been praised for the "prosperity boom" which preceded it.

When Roosevelt came up for re-election in 1930, there was no doubt about the results. Even traditionally Republican upstate New York turned out in favor of the man whose legs would no longer follow his commands. He won by 725,000 votes.

Although certain so-called financial experts were now saying that "the worst of the depression was over," and that "business was showing a healthy recovery," employment agencies were crowded to capacity with applicants, and jobs were few and far between. The funds of private welfare agencies were nearly exhausted. In certain communities there was no alternative for the destitute except the poorhouse. There were then no federal relief funds. Federal aid was considered — by those who did not need it — as degrading as the British "dole."

In an address to the State Legislature on August 28, 1931, Roosevelt made the startling statement that the government was responsible for the well-being of its people: "The duty of the state toward the citizens is the duty of the servant to his master." Citizens who had lost their means of livelihood through no fault of their own were the responsibility of the government, "not as a matter of charity, but as a matter of *social duty*."

This speech led to the allotment of money by the State Legislature for an organization which would help find jobs for the unemployed and provide food, clothing, and shelter when no jobs were forthcoming. It was called the Temporary Emergency Relief Administration, the first organization of its kind in America. As executive secretary, F.D.R. chose Harry Hopkins, a slim, intense Iowan who had spent some fifteen years doing social work in New York City slums. Soon the activities of the TERA were being repeated in other states. No one saw more clearly than Roosevelt that TERA was a temporary stop-gap which could not begin to meet the problems of the growing army of destitute persons.

In September a few of the larger newspapers

SOLD OUT

The crash of the stock market in 1929 brought
financial ruin to many middle-class families, and ...

mentioned that Japan had launched a full-scale invasion on the Chinese territory of Manchuria. One paper dismissed the matter as something for the League of Nations to handle. The story aroused indignation and pity among those who happened to read it, but America, having her own troubles, paid slight attention to it.

Roosevelt made a speech about the "forgotten man," on whom, though he was at the bottom of the "economic pyramid," prosperity must depend. Of Roosevelt's "forgotten man," Will Rogers, the American humorist, commented drily: "Every man in America thinks you were referring to him."

The Democratic Convention in Chicago, meeting in June of 1932, chose Franklin Delano Roosevelt as Presidential candidate. He flew to Chicago to accept the nomination. "I pledge you, I pledge myself, to a *new deal* for the American people," he said in his acceptance speech.

In Washington, several thousand unemployed war veterans had gathered to ask for immediate payment of their bonus, promised for 1945. When their request was refused, they camped out on Anacostia Flats with their wives and children. Following several unfortunate "incidents," federal troops drove them out with tear gas. One small baby died as a result. President Hoover, whom the Republicans had renominated for a second term, was held responsible for the mishandling of the "Bonus Marchers." His popularity shrank to a low ebb.

In the ensuing election, Roosevelt carried 42 states with a plurality of 7,000,000 votes. The "forgotten man" had voted for the "New Deal."

Some Americans noted a curious coincidence: the Democrat, Franklin Roosevelt, had followed in the footsteps of the Republican, Theodore Roosevelt — as State Senator, as Assistant Secretary of the Navy, as Governor of New York, and now as President of the United States.

...hunger and hopelessness to the dispossessed.

V. The New Deal

"The only thing we have to fear is fear itself."

On the Sunday of his Inauguration, March 4, 1933, President Roosevelt summoned the members of his new cabinet: Cordell Hull, Secretary of State; William Woodin, Secretary of the Treasury; Henry Wallace, Secretary of Agriculture; Harold Ickes, Secretary of the Interior; and the first woman to hold a cabinet post, Miss Frances Perkins, Secretary of Labor. In the Oval Room of the White House, Justice Benjamin Cardozo swore them into office. The solemn ceremony marked the opening of the promised "New Deal."

America faced a crisis as grave as a foreign invasion. The depression had passed its third winter. Fifteen million American laborers and white collar workers were seeking jobs, desperately and hopelessly. Families, unable to pay rent, lived near city dumps or other unoccupied land, in shanties made of tarpaper and packing boxes. "Hoovervilles," these wretched collections of dwellings were called.

Hunger, which cannot be seen and is hard to measure, was a living enemy. Men who had never asked charity before stood in long bread lines for a bowl of weak mush and a cup of coffee. The malnutrition rate among school children was appalling — up to 90 per cent in some schools.

Farm prices had fallen so that it hardly paid a farmer to market his products. Some of them were burning their corn rather than buying coal. They saved money that way. When foreclosures and evictions threatened, farmers gathered in grim silence to protect their own.

The national income had shrunk to less than half of what it had been four years before. Banks, unable to meet withdrawals, closed down, one after another. There were acts of violence and talk of revolution. The whole American system of government was on trial, faced with chaos.

Bonus Marchers. World War I unemployed veterans marching on Washington to demand immediate payment of their promised bonus.

*...esident Roosevelt addressing his first Congress.
...ce-President Garner is in the Speaker's Chair.
...an unrivalled "Hundred Day" session, nearly...
...the major New Deal measures were passed.*

[49]

"We must act, and act quickly," Roosevelt told the people who had put their faith in him.

His first official act was to proclaim a bank holiday. His purpose was to give bankers and the Administration a breathing space to work out legislation to restore banking on a sound basis.

"America hasn't been so happy in three years as they are today, no banks, no work, nothing," said Will Rogers. ". . . If he burned down the Capitol we would cheer and say, 'Well, we at least got a fire started anyhow.'"

Soon Americans listened to their first "Fireside Chat" from the White House. The new President spoke to them like a friend or a father. His voice was decisive, forceful, and reassuring. In the next week an avalanche of over half a million letters swamped the White House mail room. "Your human feeling for all of us in your address is just wonderful," said one. Wrote another, "People are looking to you almost as they look to God."

He called Congress for a special session on Thursday, March 9. The session lasted until June 16 — exactly one hundred days, the most remarkable one hundred days in American history.

The banking situation came first, for it was essential that the "financial arteries" of the coun-

The Brain-trusters. Left to right, Adolf Berle, Rexford G. Tugwell, Raymond Moley, with Louis Howe. F.D.R. depended on the advice of experts.

try be restored. The bill Roosevelt presented the first day of Congress gave the Secretary of the Treasury power to prevent gold hoarding and provided for review and reopening of the closed banks under a system of licenses. It was passed by four o'clock that afternoon. By Monday the banks were beginning to open again. The President had instilled such confidence in the nation that there was no frenzy of withdrawals.

Other legislation followed rapidly. On March 10, Congress passed the Economy Bill, designed to save the budget half a billion dollars. On March 13, Roosevelt obtained Congress' approval of a modification of the Eighteenth Amendment, permitting sale of light wines and beer. It was his first challenge to the many-tentacled bootlegging syndicates.

On March 16, he presented a proposal for the Agricultural Adjustment Administration — the AAA — designed to help the farmers. This was the first New Deal agency. It was followed, on March 21, by legislature to set up the Civilian Conservation Corps.

The CCC was always a favorite of Roosevelt's. At its height it gave work to half a million unemployed youths. They planted millions of trees, built truck trails, fire breaks, and soil erosion dams. They lived at camps, were paid just $30 a month, but were provided with libraries, newspapers, vocational training, dramatics, music and debating courses. The outdoor life kept them healthy. They were saved from hunger, from despair, and in some cases from crime.

On March 29, when Congress had been twenty days in session, the Securities Act was passed, paving the way for the Securities Exchange Commission — SEC — which gave government supervision of the sale of securities. On April 3, the President laid before Congress the Farm Relief Act, designed to save farm mortgages from foreclosure. On April 10, legislation for the Tennessee Valley Authority was formulated. The TVA, which launched the federal government into regional planning, was to be the most lasting of the New Deal agencies.

The Home Owners Loan Corporation — the HOLC — was approved on April 13. In May, Congress passed the Railway Reorganization Act, the Federal Relief Act, and a staggering appropriation of $3,300,000,000 for relief through public works. Next came legislation to establish the National Recovery Administration — NRA — one of the boldest of President Roosevelt's many bold experiments.

The AAA, CCC, SEC, TVA, HOLC, NRA — these were the beginning of the amazing alphabet soup with which the New Deal nourished the ailing American economy. In this remarkable "hundred days," Congress passed almost without question every measure their President proposed. It was, people said later, a real honeymoon.

From the Federal Relief Act grew the Federal Emergency Relief Administration — the FERA — which gave relief to the needy, and the Civil Works Administration—CWA—which gave work at standard wages. Harry Hopkins was director of both.

"You are to invent four million jobs in thirty days," the President told him blandly, when the CWA was launched in November, 1933. Hopkins put 4,264,000 men and women to work in time for them to have paychecks during the bitter winter of 1933-34.

CWA workers built schools, airports, playgrounds, and athletic fields, constructed roads, laid sewer pipe. CWA seamstresses made mattresses for the poor from surplus cotton. CWA teachers were employed in adult education or as instructors in rural schools which otherwise would have been closed. The program included projects for writers, artists, dancers, actors, musicians. "They've got to eat just like other people."

The CWA was succeeded by the Works Progress Administration — WPA — part of the Public Works Administration, the PWA. There was considerable bewilderment about the relationship between CWA, PWA, and WPA. Not everything went smoothly and critics invented the word "boondoggling" for projects considered useless.

There was criticism of the AAA too, particularly of its drastic measure of plowing under cotton to reduce surpluses, and of other phases of the New Deal. But there was no doubt that people had more money to spend. Unemployment was decreasing. Industry was recovering. The depression was receding.

In Washington as at Albany, Roosevelt gathered experts around him to give him advice, information, and to help him prepare his speeches. Among them were Raymond Moley, Rexford G. Tugwell, Adolf Berle, Jr., all Columbia professors; Judge Samuel Rosenman, and, later, the poet, Archibald MacLeish, and the playwright, Robert Sherwood. Louis Howe referred ironically to them as Roosevelt's brain trust. F.D.R. threw back his head and laughed. "I love it," he said. Soon newspapers coined the term "brain-truster."

Louis Howe was still his personal adviser and his closest friend, the one person Roosevelt knew he could trust to be both frank and loyal. "You thickheaded Dutchman!" Louis would cry in exasperation, when he thought Roosevelt was being obstinate. No one else would have dared such intimacy.

Missy Le Hand and Grace Tully continued to handle F.D.R.'s secretarial work. Stephen Early took over press relations, Marvin McIntyre arranged his appointments. Vice-Admiral Ross T. McIntyre became his personal physician.

While the New Dealers were taking over Wash-

The great Norris Dam was built to harness the power of the Tennessee River, part of the TVA project to restore prosperity to a devastated area.

[52]

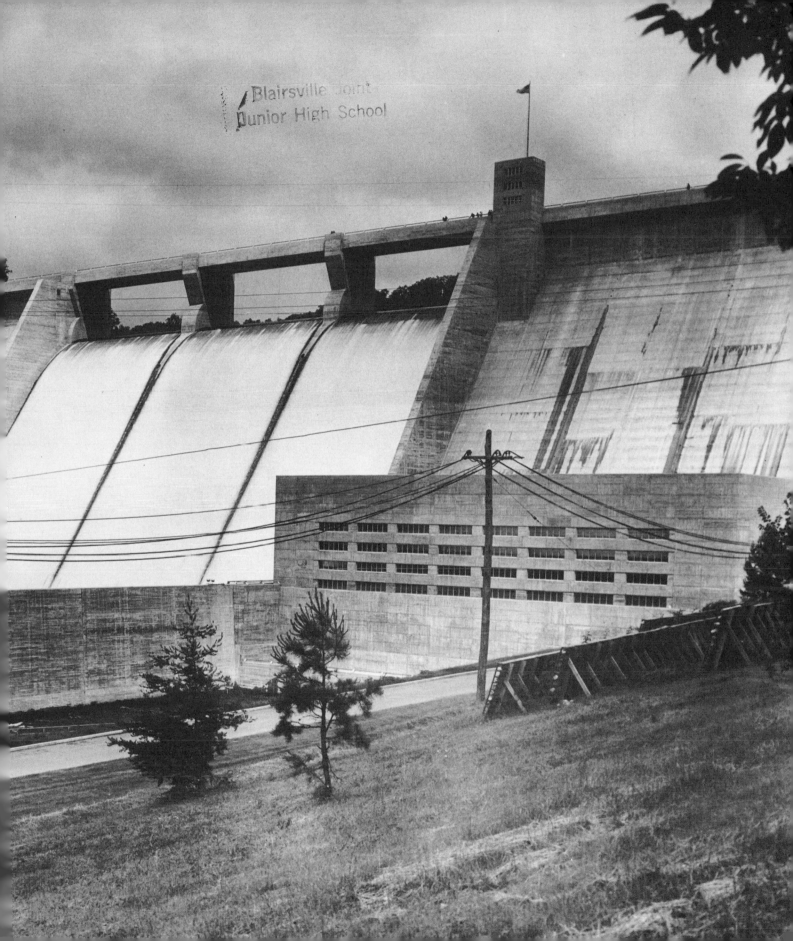

ington, the beautiful, stately White House had welcomed the lively Roosevelt family to its long list of distinguished residents. They adjusted to it not without some difficulties. The ever-present Secret Service men bothered them at first. One of the boys, returning late in a borrowed car, was almost locked out all night because he had no identification. The Roosevelt children were indignant that the White House refrigerator was kept locked at night and could not be raided.

Mrs. Roosevelt, a woman completely without pretensions, amazed the White House staff by running the elevator herself and helping the servants to move furniture.

While she mastered her many social duties as the First Lady, she did not neglect her own activities. She had her own office and her own secretary, held press conferences, and continued to write her syndicated column, "My Day." She visited prisons, hospitals, unemployed miners in a West Virginia shanty town, the back alleys of Washington and the slums of Puerto Rico. Wherever she found bad conditions, she did what she could to have them improved. She went in part because her husband wanted her to. He depended on her to find out firsthand what was happening in America. "My missis says they have typhoid in that district," he once told his cabinet members.

The veterans made a second "Bonus March" to Washington. The President gave them living quarters in a camp off Potomac Drive and arranged with the relief administration to provide them with food. Louis Howe, as the President's representative, spent long hours with their leaders. One day Howe took Mrs. Roosevelt to visit their camp. The men sang army songs for her.

Louis Howe fell ill shortly after that and was later taken to a naval hospital, where he died in 1936. Roosevelt missed him deeply. No one ever quite filled his place.

The President's "Good Neighbor Policy" was another facet of New Deal activities. "In the field of world policy I would dedicate this nation to the policy of the good neighbor," he had pledged in his Inaugural Address. Being a good neighbor meant overcoming the hostility of many Latin American or western hemisphere countries toward the all-powerful United States.

With the support of Secretary of State Cordell Hull, F.D.R. speeded up the movement begun under Hoover to withdraw marines from Haiti and to end the military occupation of Nicaragua. In Cuba, there was bitter resentment at the 1901 Platt Amendment, which had given the U.S. the right to intervene in internal dissensions and authorized acquisition of Cuban territory for American naval bases. A new agreement assured no intervention in Cuba, and that only the naval base of Guantánamo should be retained by American forces. A number of Latin American countries sent their congratulations to Roosevelt.

His appointment of Josephus Daniels, his former Navy chief, as Ambassador to Mexico improved relations in that country. When Bolivia seized certain oil properties being exploited by North American interests, the New Deal Administration, while insisting on adequate compensation, gave indication that friendly relations between the two countries took precedence over property rights. The industrialists concerned were not pleased.

Very rich people were finding other reasons to grumble about "that man in the White House." They blamed him for higher taxes and an increased federal budget, perhaps forgetting that when Roosevelt took over they had been prophesying a revolution. The family of one industrial magnate warned visitors not to mention the President's name, lest it raise the magnate's blood pressure. By the time F.D.R. had been in office two years, a "hate Roosevelt" movement, bordering on fanaticism, was under way. The President took personal attacks in his stride.

"Really, Doctor," he asked a physician one day, "do you think this carcass of mine will stand the racket awhile longer?"

"Yes, it will," the doctor assured him. "But I have a lot of high-flown Wall Street friends who are quite sure that the country cannot."

F.D.R. laughed heartily.

In 1936, the Republicans chose Alfred M. Landon, Governor of Kansas, as their Presidential candidate. The Democrats nominated F.D.R. by acclamation for a second term. His campaign train, eleven cars long, left Washington on October 8. At every whistlestop crowds gathered. They had come by wagon, car, bicycle, on foot.

He was re-elected by the greatest landslide vote in American history, carrying every state but Maine and Vermont with a total of 523 electoral votes to eight for Landon. Neither slander nor reasoned criticism had altered the adoration of the great mass of the American people for the man who had led them from disaster.

Shortly after his smashing election victory, Roosevelt sailed to South America on the *Indianapolis,* to attend the 1936 Pan-American Peace Conference in Buenos Aires. The reception with which he was greeted exceeded any ever before offered a foreign visitor. Latin Americans welcomed him, not as a hated "Yankee Imperialist," but as their friend.

For Roosevelt, a political campaign was an opportunity of making friends with the men, women and children who made up America's millions.

VI. Arsenal of Democracy

"When peace has been broken anywhere, the peace of all countries everywhere is in danger."

As Franklin Roosevelt began his second term in office, the world beyond America was splattered with the evil stains of tyranny and aggression.

Across the Pacific, the Japanese had continued their Chinese invasion, started in Manchuria in 1931, and were now occupying more than 900,000 square miles of China's territory. Bombing of civilians, burning of villages, looting and torture were the essence of their still undeclared warfare. It was plain that their ambition had grown with success and that their plans for conquest had just begun.

On the other side of the Atlantic, Mussolini's Italy had invaded Ethiopia and Franco's military forces were waging war on the existing Spanish government. In Nazi Germany, Chancellor Adolf Hitler, a little man with a clipped mustache, comical as Charlie Chaplin, had thrown into concentration camps or forced into exile thousands of German citizens because of their race, religion, or political beliefs.

Hitler screamed "German Supremacy" and "Aryan Supremacy" until outsiders were convinced he was crazy. But he had joined hands with Mussolini to form the Italo-German Axis Pact and within his own country, in defiance of the Versailles Treaty, he was building up a massive navy and air force. The Nazi *Luftwaffe,* in a "dress rehearsal" on April 26, 1937, dropped bombs on the undefended Spanish town of Guernica, killing thousands of men, women, and children.

The League of Nations was helpless.

Roosevelt regarded world events with increasing gravity. With the same certainty he had felt at the beginning of World War I, he was con-

By 1939, the Nazi Luftwaffe *had built a force of 21 squadrons and 260,000 men. Their armament industry was producing more than in the peak of World War I.*

cember 8, 1941. President Roosevelt signs the Declaration of War against Japan.

[57]

vinced that America could not forever stay clear of the tragedy overhanging other countries. He believed that, as a "good neighbor" and for her own protection, the United States should give aid to victims of lawless aggression. But he also knew how strong was the sentiment of the American people against foreign entanglements, how difficult it would be to educate them to accept responsibility as citizens of the world.

Troubles were piling up on him at home. There were his difficulties with the Supreme Court. After the Court nullified nine of eleven important New Deal measures, it seemed clear to him that several of the Court's "Nine Old Men" were sabotaging the country's welfare. In an attempt to limit their veto powers, he proposed a bill to Congress giving him the right to appoint a new judge for each Supreme Court judge who refused to retire within six months of reaching seventy. After 168 days of acrid debate, the bill was defeated. His attempt to "pack the Supreme Court" was widely criticized and for a time lost him considerable prestige.

In the Middle West, dust storms swept topsoil from millions of acres of farmland, leaving behind ground baked hard as rock. There was a new recession, for which he was blamed. Jealousies and rivalries fomented within his beloved New Deal agencies. His "honeymoon" with Congress was over. He had to fight for the legislature he thought vital — a child labor law, a minimum wage law, a new farm program.

None of these matters could keep him from devoting more and more attention to the urgency of foreign affairs. In a speech to a Chicago audience on October 5, 1937, he set out to explain to the people why they should be concerned with what was happening abroad:

"When an epidemic of physical disease starts to spread, the community approves and joins in a quarantine of the patients in order to protect the health of the community against the spread of the disease." Diseased nations, he continued, presented the same threat to healthy nations.

The "quarantine speech" brought a storm on his head. "War-mongering" and "saber-rattling" were two of the phrases used to condemn him. The reaction was not unexpected, but he was still disappointed.

"It's a terrible thing," he told Judge Rosenman sadly, "to look over your shoulder when you are trying to lead — and to find no one there."

Two months later, on December 12, Japanese war planes bombed and sank the U.S. gunboat *Panay* in the Yangtze River. The outrage stirred America as his "quarantine speech" had not. He promptly asked Congress for additional appropriations for combat ships.

The next March, the Nazis incorporated Austria as part of the German *Reich*. At Munich, on September 29, 1938, Mussolini, Edouard Daladier of France, and the English Prime Minister, Neville Chamberlain, agreed to let Hitler take over the Sudetenland from Czechoslovakia. Roosevelt

Hitler and Neville Chamberlain at Munich in September, 1938. The Munich Pact has since become synonymous with appeasement.

The King and Queen of England enjoying a sunny afternoon at Hyde Park. Mrs. Sara Roosevelt sits between the royal couple.

was distressed at Chamberlain's weakness, at his blindness for believing that the gift would keep Hitler quiet. To the Nazi Chancellor and to the Italian *Il Duce,* he sent messages, appealing for a ten-year pledge not to attack or invade other countries. It was one of many appeals, all of which he realized were futile. Hitler read Roosevelt's appeal to his *Reichstag,* who found it so funny that they laughed.

King George VI and Queen Elizabeth of England paid a good-will visit to America the next June. With war looming like a great dark giant, they knew it would be their last pleasure trip for a long time. After their official reception in Wash-

ington, the Roosevelts invited them for a weekend at Hyde Park. The Hyde Park mansion hardly compared to Windsor Castle, and Mrs. Sara Roosevelt was worried that the royal couple would have cause for complaint. On the contrary, both King and Queen were fascinated by the American way of life and the easy informality of the American President.

Roosevelt and King George went swimming together, after shooing off the inevitable horde of reporters and photographers. There was a picnic when the royal guests were introduced to traditional American fare — including hot dogs and strawberry shortcake. That evening King and

President talked until after one o'clock, when Roosevelt said paternally, "Young man, I think it's time you went to bed."

"Why don't my ministers talk to me as the President did?" George VI later demanded of the Canadian Prime Minister. "I felt exactly as though a father were giving me his most careful and wise advice."

Within a few months, on September 1, 1939, Nazi troops, on a fabricated pretext, invaded Poland. Roosevelt received the news by phone from Ambassador William C. Bullitt in Paris. "Then it's happened," said the President gravely.

Among European anti-Nazi scientists there was one burning anxiety. Did Hitler realize the potentialities of atomic power? Some seven months earlier, Lise Meitner, an Austrian refugee scientist, had discovered that uranium atoms could and were being split in laboratory experiments. The next step, the making of a device that would start atoms splitting in a chain reaction, was only a matter of time and money. Sooner or later, man would be able to harness the enormous energy of the atom — either for the benefit of mankind or for instruments of terrible destruction.

The folly of Hitler's racial policy had lost him Fräulein Meitner, Albert Einstein, and many other first-rate scientists, but Germany still had a solid core of nuclear physicists, who might or might not be willing to use their skills to develop atomic weapons, should Hitler demand that they do so. There was no way of telling what was in the mind of the *Führer,* but a group of anti-Nazi scientists in America felt that the President of the United States must be warned of the danger.

The emissary they chose was an old friend of Roosevelt's named Alexander Sachs, a New York banker and scientific amateur. He paid a visit to the White House on October 11, less than six weeks after the invasion of Poland, armed with a letter from Dr. Einstein and a memorandum from the Hungarian-born nuclear scientist, Leo Szilard.

Roosevelt hardly listened to him at first. Atomic science was one subject about which he knew next to nothing, and besides, he was preoccupied with other matters. Eventually, he grasped the significance of Sachs's visit.

"Alex," he said, "what you are after is to see that the Nazis don't blow us up."

"Precisely," Sachs told him.

Roosevelt summoned his military aide, General Edwin M. "Pa" Watson. "Pa, this requires action," he said.

From this interview stemmed the government's mighty atomic research program, started so that if Hitler did intend to develop atomic weapons, America could be one step ahead of him. That he had no such intentions, and indeed was completely indifferent to atomic affairs, was not known until years later.

The Nazis took over Norway and Denmark in April, 1940. Like some invulnerable Frankenstein monster, they stalked through Holland, Belgium, Luxemburg, bypassed the Maginot Line, and entered a weeping Paris by June 10. The Battle of Britain was under way two months later.

Roosevelt demanded that airplane production be increased to 50,000 planes a year. Munitions, sold on a cash-and-carry basis, began to seep to Great Britain, in spite of Nazi submarines. Over the Burma Road, limited supplies reached the Chinese, who were still carrying on a valiant guerrilla warfare against their invaders.

Opposition to rearmament was noisy and venomous — from the isolationists; from the German-American *Bund,* who held open meetings complete with swastikas and Hitler salutes; from certain groups who were still doing business with Hitler.

A day of tragedy. Hitler's armies in Paris goose-stepping up the Champs-Elyseés by the Arc de Triomphe.

Were the majority of the people with the President? There was only one way to find out.

F.D.R. agreed to run for an unprecedented third term only because the Democrats had no other candidate to carry on what he had started. He did not plan to campaign but changed his mind when he learned that the Republican candidate, the likable and intelligent Wendell Willkie, was making great headway. "I am an old campaigner, and I love a good fight," he said, when he took to the road again.

Fala, the most famous dog in the world. Small children sometimes wrote letters to him, convinced that, unlike most canines, Fala could read and write.

His smile and his laughter were as infectious as ever and his sarcasm as mighty, when he cared to use it. "American ostriches," he called the isolationists: "It is not good for the ultimate health of ostriches to bury their heads in the sand." Smart politician that he was, he did a most unpolitical thing by signing the first peacetime draft before, instead of after, the election. Yet once again he won, hands down, by an electoral vote of 449 to 82, taking all but 10 states.

He was fifty-eight and the past eight years had taken their toll on his health. His biggest job lay ahead.

That fall he received a delightful gift from his favorite cousin, Margaret Suckley — a small and shaggy black Scottish terrier. Fala, Roosevelt named him. Fala attended press conferences, sat on the edge of the White House pool while the President was swimming, trotted up to his master's bedroom each morning.

In January, when the President put on his overcoat and tall silk hat to go to the Capitol for his Inauguration, Fala jumped into the waiting car to go with him. Nor would the Scottie budge until Roosevelt's bodyguard, Tommy Qualters, firmly lifted him out.

Lend-Lease was a "brain wave" which Roosevelt had on a cruise some weeks after his re-election—a way in which arms and ammunition could be supplied to countries too poor to pay cash. Lend-Lease, Roosevelt explained to the American people in a "Fireside Chat," was "the arsenal of democracy."

"Suppose my neighbor's home catches fire," he told a press conference, "and I have a length of garden hose. If he can take my garden hose and connect it up with his hydrant, I may help him to put out his fire . . . I don't say to him before that operation, 'Neighbor, my garden hose cost me $15; you have to pay me $15 for it.' I don't want $15 . . . I want my garden hose back after the fire is over."

Lend-Lease, the garden hose to put out the fire in the houses of neighboring countries, was made into a bill and passed on March 11, 1941. By May, Lend-Lease material was piling up in American ports even faster than ships could carry it away. The Germans retaliated by torpedoing the American merchant ship, *Robin Moore,* stranding passengers and crew in lifeboats hundreds of miles from land. Roosevelt announced an "unlimited national emergency." On June 22, the seemingly invincible German armies invaded the Soviet Union, in violation of the Soviet-German Pact.

In August, President Roosevelt and Prime Minister Winston Churchill met secretly in foggy Argentia Harbor off the shores of Newfoundland,

President Roosevelt and Prime Minister Winston Churchill at the historic "Atlantic Charter" meeting, off the coast of Newfoundland, August, 1941.

in sessions held alternately on the *U.S.S. Augusta* and the British *H.M.S. Prince of Wales*. At last, said someone, the black cigar (Churchill's) and the cigarette in the long holder (Roosevelt's) would be lighted by the same match. F.D.R.'s sons, Elliott and Franklin Jr., members respectively of the Army Air Corps and the Naval Reserve, were present, and so was Fala.

Churchill was there to plead a desperate cause. Without America's all-out aid, the British Empire was doomed. The President also had a cause to plead. There was a condition to America's help and that was that the British change their attitude toward colonization. The "eighteenth-century methods" of taking wealth from colonial countries and giving them nothing in return, had no place in a post-war world. The peace ahead must be one where "men in all the lands may live out their lives in freedom from fear and want."

"Mr. President, England does not propose for a moment to lose its favored position among the British Dominions," Churchill said.

Roosevelt would not yield an inch.

The sparring between these two masters of

The Japanese attack on Pearl Harbor sank or damaged eight battleships and many other warcraft, destroyed hangars and planes, cost nearly 3000 casualties.

strategy continued for three days. Out of it came the historic Atlantic Charter, a blueprint of world harmony which they hoped would follow the collapse of Nazi tyranny.

The Japanese, who had formed a three-way pact with Germany and Italy, were now boldly moving southward to menace Burma, Malaya, and Singapore. Were the Philippine Islands and even the American continent next on their agenda? Would "little Japan" dare to attack the great United States? Japanese code messages, which the Navy Department had succeeded in deciphering, showed that was exactly what Japan had in mind. Roosevelt did not know when or where they would strike, but he did know it might come any time.

In the meantime he was following a course of appeasement — a word he detested. He knew it would do little good: "No man can tame a tiger into a kitten by stroking it." But until the United States could build a bigger war machine, he had no choice

The suspense ended when, on December 7, 1941, Japan attacked Pearl Harbor and, almost simultaneously, Wake, Guam, and the Philippines.

"A day which will live in infamy," the President called Pearl Harbor. The next morning, his face grim and angry, he asked a joint session of Congress to "declare that since the unprovoked and dastardly attack by Japan . . . a state of war has existed between the United States and the Japanese Empire."

The Senate passed its vote for war within half an hour. Two days later, Captain Colin P. Kelly, Jr., took off in a bomb-ladened B-17 from the Philippines, scored a direct hit on the Japanese battleship *Haruna* before his burning plane exploded. On December 11, Italy and Germany, Japan's Axis partners, declared war on the U.S.

THE WHITE HOUSE
WASHINGTON

December 17, 1941

TO THE PRESIDENT OF THE UNITED STATES IN 1956:

I am writing this letter as an act of faith in the destiny of our country. I desire to make a request which I make in full confidence that we shall achieve a glorious victory in the war we now are waging to preserve our democratic way of life.

My request is that you consider the merits of a young American youth of goodly heritage -- Colin P. Kelly, III -- for appointment as a Cadet in the United States Military Academy at West Point. I make this appeal in behalf of this youth as a token of the Nation's appreciation of the heroic services of his father who met death in line of duty at the very outset of the struggle which was thrust upon us by the perfidy of a professed friend.

In the conviction that the service and example of Captain Colin P. Kelly, Jr. will be long remembered, I ask for this consideration in behalf of Colin P. Kelly, III.

Franklin D. Roosevelt

Captain Colin P. Kelly, Jr., was posthumously awarded the Distinguished Service Cross, and a written tribute by the President.

VII. The Darkest Days

"The news is going to get worse and worse
before it begins to get better."

Two of President Roosevelt's "brain-trusters," Judge Sam Rosenman and Robert Sherwood, were walking along Pennsylvania Avenue in front of the White House the evening of December 8th. They noticed that the brilliant light beneath the White House portico was not shining. For the first time in the memory of any living American there was darkness on the White House grounds.

"I wonder how long before that light gets turned on," the Judge said thoughtfully.

Sherwood shrugged. "I don't know. But until it does, the lights will stay off all over the world."

Mrs. Henry Nesbitt, the White House housekeeper, put in an order for blackout curtains. The basement of the nearby Treasury Department was transformed into an air shelter. F.D.R. joked about this with his old friend, Henry Morgenthau, who was now Secretary of the Treasury. "Henry, I will not go down into the shelter unless you allow me to play poker with all the gold in your vaults." White House staff, residents, and guests were provided with gas masks and introduced to air raid drills.

There were other changes. The public was no longer permitted to visit the first floor of the White House. The Secret Service was enlarged. Every-

one who worked or lived there had to be fingerprinted. Gun crews were placed on the roof.

Within a few days blackout tests began in major cities along both the Pacific and Atlantic coasts. To keep ships from being silhouetted by an offshore glare, most coastal towns were dimmed out for the duration. Civilian Defense headquarters, set up some months before, were swamped by volunteers as air raid wardens, plane spotters, first aid workers, and firemen. They learned what an incendiary bomb looks like and how to put it out. A San Bernardino unit drilled in gas masks, with smoke pots to add realism to their work.

In coastal towns, blackout curtains were added to
the American housewife's budget.

w York, the "City of Bright Lights," was
dimmed out for the duration.

[67]

By the end of 1942, U.S. war factories had a headstart on the 1943 goal of 125,000 planes — one every eight and a half minutes.

On December 22, Winston Churchill arrived at the White House with his staff and his endless supply of black cigars. At this second meeting of the two world leaders, the Arcadia Conference, a painful decision was made. For the present, it was impossible to launch a concentration of forces against Japan. Germany, with its military stockpiles fattening on the wealth and slave labor from occupied lands, had to be stopped first.

On January 1, 1942, all nations fighting Hitler, including the Soviet Union, signed the Declaration of the United Nations. Roosevelt had proposed the name "United Nations." Only a few paragraphs long, this Declaration pledged to uphold the principles of the Atlantic Charter, pledged the full resources and cooperation of each country, and guaranteed that none of the signers would make a separate peace.

"The militarists of Berlin and Tokyo started this war," Roosevelt told Congress in his State of the Union Message of February 5th. "The massed, angered forces of common humanity will finish it . . . Our own objectives are clear . . . smashing the militarism imposed by war lords upon their enslaved peoples . . . liberating the subjugated nations . . . establishing and securing freedom of speech, freedom of religion, freedom from want, and freedom from fear everywhere in the world . . ."

It was not the first time he had spoken of his "Four Freedoms," but Pearl Harbor had given them a new meaning. Congress, who had so often frustrated him in the past, interrupted him frequently with wild applause.

He went on to announce the goals for wartime production: 60,000 planes, 45,000 tanks, 20,000 anti-aircraft, six million dead-weight tons of shipping for 1942; nearly double those amounts for 1943.

Even to Harry Hopkins, these figures seemed astronomical. "Oh, the production people can do it if they really try," Roosevelt assured him confidently.

The outcome of the war at this time seemed terribly uncertain.

Guam, Wake, Hongkong, Sarawak, Borneo had fallen. The Japanese had made landings in the Solomon Islands and Papua, bringing the fight to Australia's front door. They landed on the northern coast of Java on February 28th, and on March 8th took over Rangoon. They occupied Attu and Kiska in the Aleutians.

Japanese troops held all of the Philippines except for a tiny peninsula of Bataan, where General Douglas MacArthur's troops, cut off from arms, munitions, and medical supplies, were making a valiant stand. The President ordered MacArthur to Australia, in early March, as Commander of the United Forces in the Southwest Pacific. The Bataan defense collapsed on April 9th. Some

A camouflaged Japanese infantryman.

10,000 men escaped to the island fortress of Corregidor, holding out for 28 days of incessant bombardment.

"I know how a mouse feels caught in a trap," reported Private Irving Strobing of Brooklyn in the last radio message from the fortress. People wept when they read of Corregidor. Those who had been so sure that "it could not happen here," were silenced.

The one bit of good news in this bitter picture of defeat in the Pacific was the success of Jimmy Doolittle's daring and totally unexpected bomber raid on Tokyo. When a too curious reporter asked the President where the Doolittle bombers came from, he answered mysteriously, "From Shangri-La."

The first of the American Expeditionary Forces to Europe reached northern Ireland on January 25, 1942. That month, the Nazi submarines sank more than a ship a day in the Atlantic, and in February they doubled the score. From Kittery, Maine, to Miami, Florida, the sands were sodden with petroleum from tankers and the bunkers of merchantmen, mixed with shattered lifeboats, wrecked lifebuoys, and the bodies of youths who had gone forth bravely to make the world safe for democracy.

During those early days of 1942 when weapons and convoys were painfully insufficient, Air Force Machinist's Mate First Class, Donald Mason, wired a message back to headquarters: "Sighted sub; sank same." Soon all America was chanting the terse phrase. Mason was promoted and decorated with the Distinguished Flying Cross.

In lieu of victories, President Roosevelt devoted his "Fireside Chats" to stories of individual heroism, in the Pacific and in the Atlantic, in Iceland and Greenland. There was never any lack of these.

By March, the battle of production was under way, with Donald Nelson as head of the War Production Board, and over five million men — and women — actively engaged.

They worked in automobile plants, turning out tanks where a short while before pleasure cars had rolled from the assembly lines; in shipyards; in the hundred new ammunition factories which kept going 24 hours a day. They produced PT boats, sub-chasers, destroyers, machine guns, trench mortars, Garand rifles, howitzers.

There were jobs for everyone and the pay was good, but their hearts were in it and most of them worked as they never had before. At the Kaiser shipyards, workers proudly set a record by fitting out a Victory ship in four and a half days — complete with towels on the rail in the captain's cabin, a fire in the cook's galley, and even a cake baking in the oven. The time to *build* a Liberty ship was in a short time reduced from 242 days to 41.

A large proportion of war production was of the million and one things needed in a war besides weapons and ships: surgical instruments, blankets, flashlights, canteens, gas masks, screw drivers, and such miscellaneous items as toothbrushes, shoelaces and needles. The garment industry recruited its full forces to make some five million uniforms. The shoe industry used priority leather for the millions of pairs of shoes which a large army must have. Farmers and farm laborers were urged to grow more crops. America had not only to feed its armies but a good part of the world.

The United States quickly took on a wartime look. Army patrols guarded war factories, docks, bridges, and oil reserves. Anti-aircraft gun emplacements ringed major cities and industrial plants, and dotted the length of both coasts. In planes and trains, on city streets and in restaurants, theaters and nightclubs, men in uniform, on

American Expeditionary Forces marchi
in Ireland.

GEN. GEORGE C. MARSHALL

GEN. DWIGHT D. EISENHOWER

GEN. HENRY H. ARNOLD

GEN. DOUGLAS MACARTHUR

ADM. ERNEST J. KING

ADM. CHESTER W. NIMITZ

ADM. WILLIAM F. HALSEY

BRIG. GEN. THOMAS HOLCOMB

leave or headed overseas, dominated the civilian population. Women in uniform were frequent too, as the WAACS and, later, the WAVES and SPARS were organized to do detail work for Army, Navy, and Coast Guard. "Basic training" and "boot training" were common expressions which needed no explanation.

With the zeal with which he had launched the New Deal, Roosevelt set war agencies into operation. He reorganized the entire U.S. military, replacing conflicting bureaus by three supreme sections under Chief of Staff, George C. Marshall: Air Force, in the command of Lieutenant General H. H. Arnold; Ground Force, headed by General Lesley McNair; and Supply, in the command of Major General Brehon B. Somervell. For naval operations, Roosevelt had to oversee the Atlantic fleet, in the command of Admiral Ernest J. King, and the fighting forces in the Pacific, headed by Admiral Chester Nimitz.

In his triple role as President and Commander-in-Chief of Army and Navy, he was criticized for not delegating authority accurately, for giving contradictory instructions, and for playing favorites. He got things done, but it was said that he took too much on himself and worked too hard.

The month of May brought the first decisive American victories in the Pacific, at Coral Sea and Midway Island. Heavy losses to the Japanese Fleet were due to air power; neither Japanese nor U.S. ships fired a single shot from their big guns. With those victories, the era of the battleship was ended. In the shipyards, plans for five monster 60,000-ton battleships were scrapped, while others were converted to carriers.

The "Shangri-La," from which Doolittle's bombers were launched, was in reality the carrier *Hornet*. And the President had his own Shangri-La, where he could hide out when the pressure of his duties became unbearable.

All of Roosevelt's top staff had code names. General Marshall, for instance, was PEACH, *General Eisenhower was* LIME, *General Arnold* CHERRY, *and Admiral King* APPLE. *Roosevelt himself had many code names —* MAPLE, SPRUCE, BEECH, REDWOOD, ZEPHYR, *and* CITADEL.

This was a settlement of pine cabins in the Catoctin Hills in Maryland, a couple of hours' drive from Washington, which the U.S. Marines had taken over as a training camp.

The largest cabin was reserved for the President and his guests. It had a combination living and dining room, a kitchen, four small bedrooms and two baths. The furniture was plain, and the rugs were shabby, but the windows looked out over a lovely valley. A crew of Filipino boys did the housekeeping, and the rest of the President's staff stayed in outlying cabins.

Sometimes Mrs. Roosevelt accompanied her husband to Shangri-La, but more often than not she was too busy with her own war activities.

In October, 1942, she went to England, to find out about British women in the war and to carry to American servicemen a personal message of encouragement from the President. While there, she paid a return visit to the King and Queen at Buckingham Palace, where she ate war bread from a golden plate and shivered in her enormous and luxuriously furnished bedroom. Like their British subjects, the royal couple held to the war restrictions on heat, water, and food.

During her visit, long-laid plans for the first Allied offensive against Hitler and Mussolini were nearing completion. On November 8, American and British forces, in the command of a Texas-born West Pointer, Lieutenant General Dwight D. Eisenhower, made successful landings in Algeria and Morocco.

The Allies were at last on the march. The Soviets had repulsed the Nazis at Stalingrad. In Egypt, General Bernard Montgomery and his Eighth Army were forcing back German General Rommel's *Afrika Korps*. In the Pacific, the Navy smashed a vast Japanese armada off the island of Guadalcanal.

There was another American triumph which was kept "top secret." On December 2, 1942, under the west stands of Stagg Field at the University of Chicago, the world's first atomic reactor was set in operation. Many scientific minds had contributed to the reactor's success, but the presiding genius was an anti-fascist Italian, Enrico Fermi. The reactor was the first experimental proof of what Szilard and other scientists had known was possible; the harnessing of atomic energy.

Artist's conception of the first nuclear reactor, designed by Enrico Fermi, a major achievement of nuclear science.

MELVIN A. MILLER '46

VIII. Victory in Sight

*"Victory in this war is the first and greatest goal
before us. Victory in the peace is the next."*

The Casablanca Conference, held in January, 1943, was planned by Roosevelt and Churchill to discuss future war plans. The Soviet Union leader, Joseph Stalin, was invited but had asked to be excused due to his pressing duties as Commander of the Red Armies. The President arrived on a C-54 transport plane, his first airplane trip since he flew to Chicago to accept the nomination for his first term in office. It was also the first time any United States President had flown outside the United States, and the first time a President had left his country in wartime.

A more exotic setting for the meeting could not have been chosen. Casablanca, a city of shining white buildings and blooming oleanders and bougainvillea, was swarming with Nazi spies and collaborators like most of newly liberated French Morocco. The hotel and villas assigned to the official visitors were fenced in by barbed wire and patrolled by American troops. Secret Service men were everywhere.

There was, someone said, enough top brass at the Conference to outfit a battleship. The American contingent included General Marshall, Admiral King, young General Eisenhower, who had been in command of the African invasion, and

there were equally top ranking personages among the British and French staffs.

As at the Atlantic Conference, the President had arranged for his sons, Lieutenant Colonel Elliott Roosevelt and Lieutenant Franklin D. Roosevelt, Jr., USNR, to join him. This brought him some criticism, which he ignored. He loved his boys and wanted them near him whenever possible.

In her Pacific tour, Mrs. Roosevelt covered 17 islands, including Australia, totalled 25,000 miles.

*...opical Casablanca in North Africa was the set-
...g of the second major conference between Presi-
...lent Roosevelt and Prime Minister Churchill.*

[75]

Roosevelt and Churchill were "Winston" and "Franklin" to each other now. They worked well together and in spite of some differences of opinion, their friendship and mutual respect had deepened. Out of their meetings came the decision to make Sicily the next point of assault, and, when the time came, to demand "unconditional surrender" of their enemies. This, Roosevelt believed, was essential to insure future world peace.

The presence of so many strangers did not escape the Nazis, and there was some danger of an air attack. It was suggested that they move the Conference to inland Marrakech. The President firmly refused. He also wanted very much to visit the Algerian front, but his staff begged him not to tempt fate any further. He did go out in a jeep to view American troops stationed north of Rabat.

One evening he talked with Sultan Sidi Mohammed of Morocco about the problems facing the Moroccan people. The Sultan came bearing gifts, including a beautiful gold tiara for Mrs. Roosevelt. The President accepted it gravely, not mentioning that he had the kind of wife who would never in a thousand years wear a gold tiara in public.

"I'm a bit tired — too much plane," he wrote her on his return journey. From then on tiring plane trips to far places were a regular part of his life's pattern.

Back at home he found Fala, wagging his tail delightedly to see his master once more — and a monstrous load of unfinished tasks.

The elegant Madame Chiang Kai-shek, wife of China's generalissimo, paid the Roosevelts a visit in February. He made an inspection trip through the nation's war plants and training camps that spring. He had to intervene in a rubber industry strike in Akron, and he tried to persuade John L. Lewis, president of the United Mine Workers, to submit labor difficulties to the War Labor Board, to prevent a production-crippling coal strike.

In the America of 1943, unemployment had almost vanished. The number of working women had increased by nearly 50 per cent. Farmers, who had suffered first from the depression and then from droughts and dust storms, were in clover, so to speak; their purchasing power had doubled since 1939.

There was plenty of money around but some restrictions as to how it might be spent. Pleasure driving was out for the duration of the war. Gasoline was strictly rationed, and tires, like other rubber products, were available only for essential

President Roosevelt conferring with the King of Arabia.

Red Cross girls supplied American GI's with welcome refreshments in all the theaters of the war.

needs. Sugar and coffee were the first foodstuffs to be rationed. On March 1, rationing was set up for processed foods, and soon thereafter for meats and fats. In spite of everything, Americans were by far the best fed people in the world.

The making of radios for civilians was banned, and production was halted or drastically curbed on such varied items as lawnmowers, typewriters, safety razors, garden tools, luggage, cosmetics, furniture, and zippers. A maximum skirt length was set for women's clothing, and men's suits were made without trouser cuffs and patch pock-

ets. But to foreign visitors, American stores were castles of abundance.

Almost everyone wanted to do his or her share in the war effort, some from the pure and lofty motive of patriotism, some because they would have felt out of things if they hadn't. Blood donors by the thousands reported to the Red Cross to meet a goal of a million pints for transfusions at war hospitals — and gave over 13 million. Thousands of women served in the American Women's Voluntary Service. There were Bundles for Britain drives, War Bond balls, parties for

President Roosevelt decorating General Mark Clark in Sicily.

China or Russian War Relief. Girl Scouts, with bicycles hitched to old toy express wagons, made salvage rounds for metal and rubber or collected books and magazines for overseas USO clubhouses.

Book sales mounted and best sellers included Wendell Willkie's *One World,* Joseph E. Davies' *Mission to Moscow, Here Is Your War* by war correspondent Ernie Pyle, *The Moon is Down* by novelist John Steinbeck. The flood of war books, mostly non-fiction, was just beginning.

Motion picture goers saw realistic documentaries, *The Battle of Britain, Desert Victory, In Which We Serve,* or more romanticized war films, like *Mrs. Miniver* with Greer Garson. The war theme was prevalent in radio dramas, some of high literary quality such as the plays of Stephen Vincent Benét and Edna St. Vincent Millay's *The Murder of Lidice,* the story of the Czechoslovakian village that was "liquidated" in revenge for the assassination of the Nazi "hangman," Reinhard Heydrich.

People were making jokes about the Pentagon in Washington, the largest office building in the world. General Arnold, it was said, traversed the vast corridors on a motor scooter. There was also the one about the Western Union boy who was lost in the building for three weeks and emerged a colonel.

The wounded of Guadalcanal were being brought back to hospitals on the Pacific coast, carrying the burden of gruesome and unforgettable memories of jungle warfare.

Thirty-five miles northwest of Santa Fe, New Mexico, on the 7300-foot-high Los Alamos Mesa of the Pajarito, a city of wooden barracks and tar-papered dormitories had grown up almost overnight. One by one, there arrived American and foreign scientists of world renown, Enrico Fermi, Niels Bohr from Denmark, Hans Bethe from Germany, Sir James Chadwick from England, and many others. Their identities were kept a strict secret. Fermi was known as "Henry Farmer," and Niels Bohr was "Nicholas Baker." The people in the valley couldn't imagine what was going on there. Some thought that maybe a space ship was being made. A humorist suggested the product was windshield wipers for submarines. No one guessed that this would be the home of the first atomic bomb.

Roosevelt and Churchill had another meeting in August at Quebec, where it was decided to create a Southeast Asia Command under Lord Louis Mountbatten, with General Joseph W. Stilwell as Deputy Supreme Allied Commander in the area. In a joint statement they gave the good news that the British and United States Navies now had the upper hand in the war against German U-boats.

From Quebec, the President went to Ottawa to speak to the Canadian people: ". . . I am everlastingly angry only at those who assert vociferously that the Four Freedoms and the Atlantic Charter are nonsense because they are unattainable. If those people had lived a century and a half ago they would have sneered and said that the Declaration of Independence was utter piffle..."

Early in October, Roosevelt, in a message to Congress, promised independence to the Philippines as soon as possible after the Japanese were expelled. The promise bolstered the morale of the courageous Philippine guerrilla fighters. As he made it, perhaps Roosevelt remembered his debate at Groton so many years before: "Resolved that the Philippines should have their independence..."

The bitterness of the veterans returning from the First World War was also a vivid memory, and it seemed to Roosevelt that in this war the

men deserved more than a few dollars in the form of bonuses or handouts. His thinking led to the forming of the G.I. Bill of Rights, whereby veterans would have a chance to make up for the education they had missed, a chance to improve their skills or learn a new profession.

He was concerned about the people in occupied countries who would still face hunger and want after their liberation. On November 9, he called a meeting at the White House, where representatives of forty-four nations signed an agreement for a world organization dedicated to restoring liberated peoples to health and normal lives. United Nations Relief and Rehabilitation Administration, it was called.

Four days after the birth of UNRRA Roosevelt was on his way to Teheran, the capital of

President Roosevelt reviews troops in North Africa. In the rear of the jeep is General Dwight Eisenhower.

President Roosevelt in the Pacific, July, 1944. Tokyo is the target of Admiral Nimitz's pointer.
Seated left to right, *General Douglas MacArthur, F.D.R., Admiral William D. Leahy.*

Iran, for the first conference of the "Big Three," himself, Churchill and Stalin. Roosevelt had been curious to know what "Uncle Joe," as he privately called the Soviet leader, was like. He found a man short in stature but of powerful build with graying hair and drooping mustache, dressed in his marshal's gray uniform. In repose, his face was enigmatic; on occasion he broke out in a rapturous smile.

The President got along well with "Uncle Joe," as he did with almost anyone he set his mind to charm. Relations between Stalin and Churchill were also cordial on the surface at first. Later, as differences arose between the Britisher of aristo-

cratic background and the Russian son of a shoe cobbler, Roosevelt acted in the role of mediator.

Out of the Teheran Conference came plans for the "Second Front," which the starving people of occupied Europe had awaited with desperate longing. The massive assault was made on the Normandy coast of France, across the Channel from England, on June 6, 1944.

"D-Day," as this mighty assault was called, was the greatest air and sea force ever assembled in one spot — four thousand ships timed to arrive almost simultaneously along the 50-mile Normandy beachhead; 2000 transport planes and gliders; the thickest anti-submarine patrols the

[80]

world had ever seen; a million men — under the invasion Supreme Commander, General Dwight D. Eisenhower.

By August 19, General Patton's tanks were in the suburbs of Paris. On the 25th, the French and American forces entered the city, to be welcomed by the cheering, laughing, sobbing population.

In the Pacific, United States troops had captured Saipan and Guam and made a landing on Tinian. There was some criticism of the Navy's "island hopping" by armchair generals at home, but the strategy later proved sound. U.S. troops also had retaken Attu in the Aleutians. For a week they bombarded Kiska, the other Japanese holding in the Aleutians, but when they finally landed found it vacated except for two lonely dogs.

Roosevelt was in Hawaii in July, 1944, for a conference with Admiral Nimitz. While there, he visited the war hospitals, and in wards where there were amputées, insisted that he be rolled in on his wheelchair.

There was a soldier who had amputated his own legs on the battlefield. "Good morning, Doctor," Roosevelt greeted him. "I understand you're quite a surgeon. Well, I happen to be a pretty good orthopedist myself." He was smiling and the youth grinned back at him, but when the President was wheeled out his eyes were filled with tears.

He returned to America via the Aleutian Islands and Alaska. His third term was drawing to a close. That the Democrats nominated him for a fourth — with Harry S. Truman as his running mate — aroused no protests at all.

Teheran Conference, November, 1943. The first meeting of the "Big Three" — Stalin, Roosevelt, and Churchill.

IX. Fourth Term

*"I never forget that I live in a house owned by all the
American people and that I have been given their trust."*

Roosevelt had not intended to spend time campaigning, but as in his third term, he changed his mind. It seemed to him that some of the things the opposition was saying about him and his Administration needed disproving.

In a Philadelphia speech, he challenged certain Republican orators who were charging that the present Administration was "the most spectacular collection of incompetent people who ever held public office."

"Well, you know, that is pretty serious," F.D.R. drawled, "because the only conclusion to be drawn from that is that we are losing this war. If so, that will be news to most of us — and it will certainly be news to the Nazis and the Japs."

To the Teamster's Union at the Statler Hotel in Washington, he read a paragraph from the Republican Party platform, saying that they accepted "the purposes of the National Labor Relations Act, the Wage and Hour Act, the Social Security Act, and all other federal statutes designed to promote and protect the welfare of the American working men and women . . ."

He was not going to let them get away with that. It was these very laws that many Republican leaders "have personally spent years of effort and energy — and much money — in fighting . . ."

The climax of his Teamster's Union speech was his defense of his little dog Fala, about whom a ridiculous story had popped up, to the effect that the President had left him behind on his visit to the Aleutians and had sent a destroyer back for him — at a cost of some millions of dollars to taxpayers.

"These Republican leaders have not been content with attacks on me, or my wife, or on my sons . . . they now include my little dog Fala . . . I don't resent attacks, and my family doesn't resent attacks, but Fala does resent them . . ."

Roosevelt with his daughter, Anna Roosevelt Boettiger.

*triumphal return, February, 1945. Members
the 503rd Parachute Infantry Regiment jump
a field on Corregidor, where the Americans had
suffered their cruelest defeat.*

The Fala incident possibly did more to harm the Republican candidate, Governor Thomas Dewey of New York, than anything else in the campaign. "Roosevelt's dog got Dewey's goat," people quipped.

In this campaign, as in all others, F.D.R. was careful never to speak against Republicans, but only against "certain Republican leaders." From experience he knew that there were progressive Republicans, just as there were reactionary Democrats. In recent months, he had considered uniting with Wendell Willkie, whom he greatly admired, to form a new party which would draw from the progressive ranks of both the other parties. But Willkie died on October 8, 1944, before they had a chance to discuss the matter.

Roosevelt was in New York on October 21, the day after the triumphant landing of American troops in the Philippines. Millions of New Yorkers lined the streets to catch a glimpse of their President. It was cold and raining, and his physician urged him to cancel his outdoor appearance.

Roosevelt, on the contrary, welcomed the bad weather. It gave him a splendid chance to scotch the rumor that he was too ill and old to be President. In his open car, with his navy cape over his shoulders, he drove fifty miles through the city in the pouring rain. To the waiting crowds, he waved and smiled with the all-embracing Roosevelt friendliness. Never had he seemed more indestructible. Several of his party came down with colds afterwards. The President suffered no bad effects at all.

For all the wild applause that greeted him wherever he made an appearance, the political tide was turning. The election returns gave him thirty-six states, but only 25,600,000 electoral votes, compared to 22,000,000 for Dewey. For his wartime Inauguration, he insisted upon a simple ceremony. A reporter asked him if there was

The "mopping up" job on Corregidor. After the America

to be a parade. He shook his head. "Who is there here to parade?" he asked sadly.

The year 1944 ended with furious fighting at the Ardennes — the Battle of the Bulge. "The enemy is making his supreme effort," said General Eisenhower.

ad taken the island, Japanese hid out in shell holes and caves, a dangerous prey to be approached with caution.

Some 12,000,000 American men were in uniform, stationed in all parts of the globe — 8,000,000 in the Army and approximately 4,000,000 in the Navy, Marine Corps and Coast Guard — uprooted from their homes and separated from those who loved them. American casualties were mounting toward the grim final total of nearly a million, 20 per cent killed, 50 per cent wounded, the rest missing or prisoners of war.

On the home front, there were still signs of prosperity. Restaurants were crammed. It was

hard to get a hotel room in any city. New England mill towns showed newly painted houses and freshly repaired fences. But from one end of the country to the other there was fear and anxiety in the faces of the women whose husbands, sons, brothers, or sweethearts were far away and in danger. A restlessness was in the air, which high wages did not ease, and a great yearning to have the long war over and done with.

On January 22, 1945, Roosevelt left Washington, secretly as always, for Yalta in the Russian Crimea. His daughter Anna was with him. She had been living in the White House for most of the past year, devoting herself to looking after her father and to working with him.

The Yalta Conference, the second meeting of the "Big Three," was set in Russia because the Soviets were engaged in their major offensive against Germany, and Stalin was hesitant to leave the Russian boundaries. Roosevelt's advisers tried to persuade him not to go, both for reasons of his health and because he was needed at home, but he went because he counted on this conference to work out plans for his most cherished dream — a permanent world peace.

The "Big Three" held eight formal meetings and many informal ones. At Yalta, the term "unconditional surrender," as it was to apply to Germany, was spelled out. It would not mean destruction or enslavement of the German people. It would mean temporary control and occupation by the four great powers (France was to be included), each to have a separate zone; the end of Nazism and the Nazi Party; the end of militarism in Germany; speedy and severe punishment for Nazi war criminals; German reparations.

The United Nations was a major point on their agenda. The voting procedure was established. The date of April 25, 1945, was set for the United Nations Conference in San Francisco, the meet-

D-Day. Troops of the 5th Engineers Special Brigade wading through the surf to the northern coast of France, at Fox Green, Omaha Beach.

ing that would launch this organization so dear to President Roosevelt's heart.

Stalin promised that the Soviet Union would declare war on Japan within two or three months after the end of the war in Europe (an advance of several months earlier than set in the Teheran Conference). In return, he asked for certain territorial rights "violated by Japan in 1904." This part of the discussion had to be kept secret, since Japan must not know what they were planning. Nonetheless, Roosevelt later was severely criticized for his "secret agreements" with Stalin.

Military experts at this time estimated that the Japanese war could not be won before the end of 1946, and not before a devastating cost in men and materiel. Already the scientists at Los Alamos were completing plans for the first test atomic explosion, to be held on a desolate desert area in southern New Mexico on July 16, 1945. The President could not know, any more than they did, whether the experiment would be a success.

The Yalta Conference, with stops at Cairo to confer with Generalissimo Chiang Kai-shek, and

The second "Big Three" conference was held at Yalta. Roosevelt, in his navy blue cloak, looks tired and haggard, after the long voyage.

Troops on Utah Beach take shelter behind sea wall while awaiting orders to move inland.

at Malta, kept him away from Washington a full five weeks. The physical and mental strain left him exhausted and listless. Nor did he quickly recover.

When he made his report on Yalta to Congress on March 1, he mentioned his infirmity for almost the first time in any public address:

"I hope that you will pardon me for this unusual posture of sitting down but I know that you will realize that it makes it a lot easier for me not to have to carry about ten pounds of steel around on the bottom of my legs; and also because of the fact that I have just completed a fourteen-thousand-mile trip."

[89]

His usual vibrant, vigorous manner was lacking. He spoke haltingly.

On April 12, 1945, he was at Warm Springs, in his six-room clapboard cottage known as the Little White House. His morning newspaper brought him good news on both fronts. The U.S. Ninth Army was within fifty-seven miles of Berlin. One hundred and fifty Super Fortresses had bombarded Tokyo in a two-hour daylight raid.

That evening he was planning to attend an outdoor barbecue at the invitation of the Mayor of Warm Springs. Toward noon an artist, Madame Elizabeth Shoumatoff, was ushered into the President's cheery living room. She had been commissioned to do his portrait. Two of his cousins were present, Laura Delano and Margaret Suckley, who had given him Fala. Miss Suckley was crocheting and Miss Delano was filling vases with flowers. Suddenly the President raised his left hand to his temple and then let it fall.

"Did you drop something?" Margaret Suckley asked him.

So quietly that no one else heard him, he said, "I have a terrific headache." Then he slumped in his chair.

Those were his last words. The doctors diagnosed a massive cerebral hemorrhage. He died within three hours without regaining consciousness.

In Washington, D.C., Eleanor Roosevelt was attending a charity concert. A phone message was handed her from Steve Early, White House

The Franklin D. Roosevelt Library, several hundred yards from the Hyde Park mansion, is now part of the National Archives and open to the public.

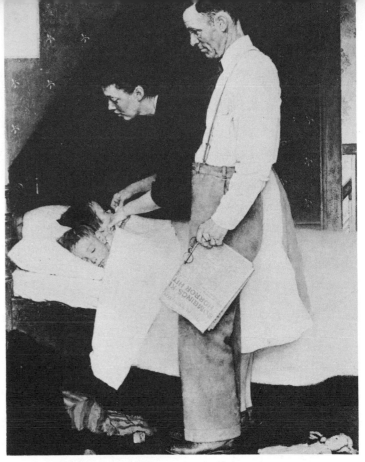

Freedom of Speech   ROOSEVELT'S FOUR FREEDOMS   *Freedom from Fear*

Freedom from Want   *Paintings by Norman Rockwell.*   *Freedom of Religion*

Head of Roosevelt — by sculptor Jo Davidson.

Press Secretary, asking her to come home at once. Intuitively she guessed the reason. Somehow she forced herself to listen until the pianist who was playing had finished the piece, then she excused herself graciously. In the car, all the way to the White House, she sat with clenched hands.

In Tokyo, Japan, a radio announcer read the bulletin of the American President's death and said, "We now introduce a few minutes of special music in honor of the passing of this great man." In beleaguered Berlin, Joseph Goebbels, Nazi propaganda minister, telephoned Adolf Hitler.

"My Führer," he said, "I congratulate you! Roosevelt is dead. It is written in the stars that the second half of April will be the turning point for us."

"I felt as if I had been struck a physical blow," Winston Churchill described his first reaction to the news. Moscow newspapers broke their rule that foreign news should appear only on the back pages of their papers. The announcement of Roosevelt's death and his picture were given front page space.

In America, Roosevelt's America, disbelief was followed by deepening sorrow. Hardened newspapermen and high cabinet officials wept openly. As the train carrying his body to Washington passed through a cotton field, Negro women sharecroppers dropped to their knees, clasping their hands together in the gesture of prayer. On New York's Rivington Street, the same street where Eleanor Roosevelt as a young woman had taught slum children dancing and calisthenics, someone asked a housewife if she had a radio. "For what would I need a radio?" she cried out. "It's on everybody's face."

Playwright Robert Sherwood visited Harry Hopkins, who was ill in bed, to talk of the man they had both known and loved so well.

"Now we've got to get to work on our own," Hopkins said. "We've had it too easy all this time, because we knew *he* was there."

Enrico Fermi, J. Robert Oppenheimer, Gener Leslie R. Groves, three leading figures in the Ma hattan Project to develop atomic energy.

Two months and four days after Roosevelt's dea July 16, 1945, the world's first atomic bomb w exploded on a desert area in southern New Mexic

[92]

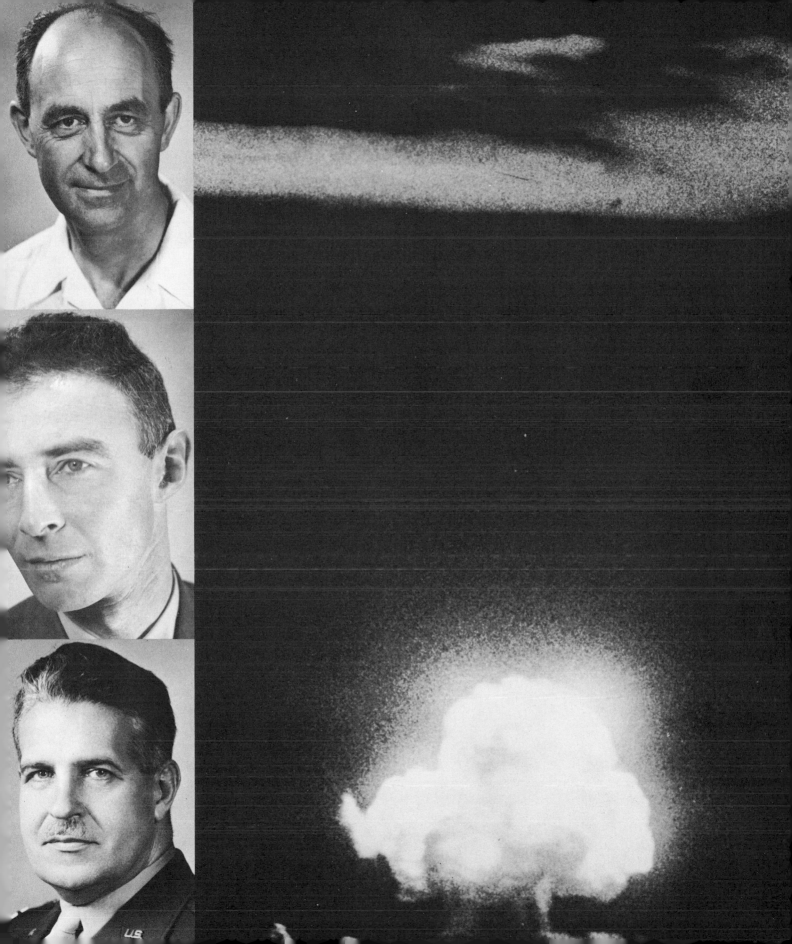

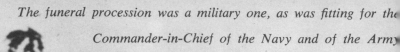

Vrote William S. White,
It was a march . . . too solemn for tears."